The Thirty-fourth Issue
of the Saturday Book

The Saturday Book

1941-1975

The Saturday Book

EDITED BY JOHN HADFIELD

34

Clarkson N. Potter, Inc./Publisher   NEW YORK

DISTRIBUTED BY CROWN PUBLISHERS, INC.

The frontispiece is adapted from an engraving in *Traité Général du Commerce*
by Samuel Ricard, 1705 (by courtesy of E. M. Lawson & Co.).

Introduction

FIRST OF ALL, a note explaining the non-appearance in 1974 of this thirty-fourth issue of THE SATURDAY BOOK. This was brought about by the crisis which hit the British industrial economy in January and February of that year. Printers and blockmakers and bookbinders were compelled, like all other industrial concerns, to operate what became known as a 'three-day week'. Whether this meant the elimination of Saturday from the week is an interesting subject for metaphysical discussion. But, in more practical terms, it meant that the timetable of producing THE SATURDAY BOOK, which involved despatch of copies to buyers in such far-distant places as the United States, Australia, New Zealand and South Africa by midsummer, became impossible of realization. An astonishing number of booksellers and regular readers wrote to say how much they missed the book.

Secondly, it is the Editor's sad duty to record the deaths of two men whose names will always be linked with THE SATURDAY BOOK. Leonard Russell, who 'founded' the book, in the second year of the Second World War, died in the autumn of last year. He was a distinguished literary editor, whose work was known (if not necessarily recognized as his) to the multitudinous readers of the London *Sunday Times*. He had a finger in several literary pies, including one actually called *Pie*, and he edited several books. But it was probably as the originator of THE SATURDAY BOOK that he best expressed himself.

In his Introductory Note to the first issue, published in 1941, Leonard set out certain aims which have, we hope, remained constant. 'The storm of the times', he wrote, 'is absent from this miscellany . . . If anything it looks backward, and nostalgia for small pre-war pleasures emerges from the pages . . . Here, then, is a tranquil book without a thunderclap of any kind.'

Leonard pursued these aims with masterly deftness and sensibility through eleven years, in the course of which he enlisted as contributors most of the eminent writers of the time, pioneered – among other things – the vogue for Victoriana, and, with the invaluable aid of Laurence Scarfe and the late Edwin Smith, created a new concept of the illustrated book.

There was a memorial service for Leonard Russell in Fleet Street's church of St Bride on Thursday, November 7, 1974 – a service that beautifully reflected his life-long devotion to the written word. Many writers gathered to commemorate him and express their affection for his widow, Dilys Powell, herself a frequent SATURDAY BOOK contributor in early days.

One of Leonard's discoveries was a bookseller's runner, Fred Bason, a sparrow-sized Cockney, collector of autographs and cigarette cards, inveterate first-nighter, gambler on 'the dogs', and diarist. In the course of time, with Leonard's encouragement, he became an entertaining and idiosyncratic talker on radio and lecturer to women's clubs, an authority on London street games, and the author of three volumes of his Diary, edited respectively by L. A. G. Strong, Nicolas Bentley and Sir Noël Coward. This irrepressible character died suddenly, whilst staying with one of his several parson friends, just as the last issue of THE SATURDAY BOOK went to press. It carried on its last page a photograph of Fred, in his cloth cap, standing in one of the South London street markets he knew so well.

Fred was buried in the churchyard at Orton Waterville, near Peterborough, where his fame as 'a modern Pepys' is recorded on a tombstone which his architect friend Lesslie Watson commissioned from the sculptor David Kindersley. Later there was a memorial service for Fred in a church off the Old Kent Road, at which another friend, Peter Gray, read passages from the famous diaries to a number of faithful S.B. devotees.

If there is an elegiac note about this Introduction it is primarily because the passage of time has seen the passing of some of the pioneers (though Olive Cook and Laurence Scarfe are still with us in these pages). Another elegiac influence is uncertainty about the future of THE SATURDAY BOOK itself, since the appalling rise in the costs of printing, paper and binding, especially the cost of colour illustration, is tending to price the book out of the market. Whether we can afford to come out next year – or you can afford to buy us – remains to be seen; but it seems more than likely that this is the last SATURDAY BOOK.

But both of those ebullient spirits, Leonard and Fred, would have deplored the shedding of tears – over their own departure or even over the end of THE SATURDAY BOOK's fantastically long run of thirty-four issues. This thirty-fourth issue therefore is devoted, as ever, to the livelier aspects of nostalgia, to the higher-spirited forms of popular art, and to some visual jokes.

Its founder, in the Introduction to the first issue, promised to hymn such pleasures as 'days by the sea, country drives, and birds, beasts and flowers'. The present editor recollects that twice he happened to write his introductory notes lying naked in a *calanque* on the island of Porquerolles, and once on the rocks below the legendary home of Circe on the Italian coast. This year he is writing in a narrow boat on the Oxford Canal, tied up by an eighteenth-century hump-backed bridge alongside, a disused Branch Railway line, with pussy willows in golden flower, and moorhens and water voles swimming stealthily among the reeds. The scene is tranquil. There is a slight meadow mist before the eyes. There are no thunder-claps.

J.H.

Contents

POPULAR ARTS

Grimaldi's Farewell Performance: Drawing by George Cruikshank

Pantomime

BY GEORGE SPEAIGHT

THERE EXISTS in Britain – and only in Britain – a unique and extraordinary kind of theatrical entertainment. Largely ignored by intellectuals, it is enormously popular, attracting large audiences in provincial cities, mainly of comparatively unsophisticated theatregoers who probably never go to any other form of theatre in their lives. It is basically traditional, but it has changed continually over the centuries, absorbing every new manifestation of popular taste; it is regarded as a children's entertainment, but it is often spiced with *risqué* jokes that only their parents can understand; it is always said to be dying, but never dies. It is the Christmas pantomime.

In an attempt to study this illogical form of drama and to find out what it is really like today, I undertook a tour of England during January during the past two years, watching pantomimes in towns all over the country and in all kinds of theatres. If I have counted right, I have seen twenty-four different productions, including *Jack and the Beanstalk* six times!

The basic pattern of a pantomime is fairly constant wherever you go. When the curtain rises a fairy will enter from the stage right, wave her wand and announce the theme in rhyming couplets. It may be a giant who terrorizes the land, a magician who plots villainy, or a wicked uncle who has designs on his wards; whatever it may be, the fairy will proclaim her aim to frustrate the evil and protect the good. But there then enters on the stage left, in a green spotlight, a demon king or a bad fairy, who will threaten ruin and terror, snarling his way through a few more rhyming couplets which will be inaudible through the boos and hisses of the audience, who know from the first what is expected of them.

The front cloth then rises to reveal a market place or village green, or perhaps a street in old Pekin, with villagers dancing and singing and often a special number by a troupe of child performers from the local dancing school. There then enters a most surprising figure, a man dressed up as a woman – the Dame. He (she) promptly ignores the story, plants himself at the front of the stage where a microphone has now often replaced the footlights, and proceeds to 'warm the audience up'. He will probably start by welcoming the parties visiting the theatre for that performance – the Little Muggins Women's Institute, the St Stephen's church choir, and so on – and at each name the party welcomed will announce their presence by a hearty cheer.

The Dame will then ask the boys and girls if they are enjoying themselves, to which they invariably reply with a hearty and uncritical 'Yes', to which he will invariably reply 'Well, you'd better leave now because it gets worse later on', and he proceeds to tell some jokes distantly or not at all connected with the story. Here are some authentic examples from last year's pantomimes, garnered from Birmingham, Coventry and Newcastle:

'My boy, Jack, is teacher's pet, you know. She keeps him in a cage at the back of the class.' [I heard that three times.]

'I'm plagued with rats, so I went to [a local store] to ask for some rat poison. The man said "Have you tried Boots?" I told him I didn't want to kick them.'

'The people up at [a smart local residential suburb] talk awful posh, you know. A lady went into [a local store] and asked for some peppah. The man said "Do you want black pepper or white pepper?" She answered "I want toilet peppah." '

Sometimes there will be a foil to the Dame, a Simple Simon or (in *Aladdin*) Wishy Washy, and we can have a dialogue with perhaps some of the vulgarities which so distress high-minded people. Here are a few more authentic examples, this time from Oldham, Leeds and Nottingham:

'My boy's learning his three Rs: reading, 'righting and 'rithmetic. So he'll always have his Rs to fall back on.'

'When my Jack had a little baby sister he asked his Daddy whether she'd been brought by a stork down the chimney. No, his Daddy said, she'd come from a lark in a field.'

'I call this my religious jersey,' says the Dame, showing a very low-cut dress, 'because it's "Lo and behold".' And then one of her 'breasts' is sure to get dislodged and turn up sticking out of her backside.

Surprisingly, perhaps, these jokes always seem to raise a good laugh. But it is time for the next principal character to appear, and this time it is a girl in tights and trunks, playing the part of a man – the Principal Boy. She (he) then sings a song, usually a popular love ballad of the season, and she will be joined by a girl – a real girl this time – who may be a Princess, or a wood-cutter's daughter, or a pretty persecuted youngest sister, but who will certainly be in love with the Principal Boy.

The story then begins to take its course. It may be *Cinderella* or *Jack and the Beanstalk*, *Aladdin* or *Dick Whittington*, *Robinson Crusoe* or *Babes in the Wood*, *Mother Goose* or *Puss in Boots*; there are only about a dozen familiar nursery tale subjects that constitute the panto-mime repertory today, but to tell the truth it doesn't much matter what the story is, somehow or other a number of tried and traditional scenes will be worked in.

One of these will be a chase. The set will have two doors and a window; the guards or policemen chase the Dame who runs out of one door and in at the next with such rapidity that soon she is chasing them; and then she disappears down the trapdoor and pops out of the window and you realize that there are two if not three Dames involved through the use of 'doubles'.

Another favourite (though, sadly, not so common now) is a 'slosh scene', with custard pies or wallpaper paste being splashed into the faces of characters, who then sit on their hats, or tread in the glue pot, or fall into the bath.

Or there may be a comic motor car that falls apart in a caco-phany of steam and explosions; or the broker's men carrying the furniture out of the Dame's house; or the Chinese laundry in *Aladdin*, with someone sure to get pushed between the rollers of the mangle and coming out as thin as cardboard. The Dame will probably find an excuse to undress, revealing layers of petticoats and corsets and scarlet drawers; and she will appear carrying a long, long washing line across the stage, festooned with the most improbable underclothes in the colours of the local football team, and then surprisingly re-appear at the other end of it.

In the course of all this the audience will play their part by shouting 'Look behind you' when a skeleton appears or a spider is let down; or indulging in an interminable dialogue of 'Yes you did', 'No you didn't' with someone on the stage.

And somewhere or other a travelling troupe of acrobats or performing dogs will appear, or a ventriloquist or a puppet master will perform, or golliwogs dance a ballet, or beautiful scenery reveal itself, or – recently – a pop group or a television star intrude. And, of course, a horse or a cow or a goose with actors inside.

Between all this the story thinly makes its way until the giant is killed, or the babes rescued, or the glass slipper fitted on to Cinderella's foot. Then comes the song sheet scene, with a big cloth carrying the words of some popular song lowered from the flies, and the Dame encouraging everyone to sing it, often dividing the audience into two in competition with each other.

After this the cloth goes up to disclose a gawdy scene with a flight of steps, and all the characters walk down it in their most beautiful costumes and in ascending order of importance, concluding always with the Principal Boy and Girl. And we all clap and cheer, and somebody makes a speech saying 'If you've enjoyed the show tell your friends; if you haven't keep your mouth [gob in Lancashire] shut.'

*   *   *   *   *

What can be the origin of such an illogical form of entertainment? Its roots lie in the bastard progeny of the Italian Commedia dell'Arte which sprang up all over Europe in the seventeenth century, and perhaps particularly in the mimed Arlequin dances of the Paris fairs.

This art soon spread to England. The stages of its development are much disputed, but by 1728 the new species of entertainment was sufficiently well established for a dancing master called John Weaver to write an account of it in a book called *The History of the Mimes and Pantomimes*. During the eighteenth century this form of entertainment developed into a mixture of ballet and mime, with some spoken dialogue, some songs, some topical or political satire, some knock-about farce, and some trick scenic effects. The basic theme was often based on classical mythology but sometimes on native folk legend or contemporary events, and through it all the characters descended from the Italian Comedy mimed, joked and danced their incongruous way. A random selection of titles will give some indication of the subject matter: *Amadis, or The Loves of Harlequin and Columbine* (1718), *The Necromancer, or Harlequin Doctor Faustus* (1723), *Harlequin Invisible, or The Emperor of China's Court* (1724), *The Fairy Queen, or Harlequin turn'd Enchanter by Magic Art* (1730). These were all afterpieces, not the main item in the evening's programme, and neither specifically intended for children nor associated with Christmas. They were much attacked by critics and serious dramatists, but they were enormously popular. A new form of theatrical entertainment had been born, and it has remained popular in England ever since.

Early in the nineteenth century the style of pantomime was transformed by the development of the character of Clown in the hands of 'Joey' Grimaldi. The show now took the form of an Opening, based on some legendary or historical theme and spoken in rhyming couplets, at the end of which the principal characters were changed in a 'transformation scene' into the characters of the Harlequinade – Harlequin, Columbine, Clown and Pantaloon. This Harlequinade became the most important element in the show, with the introduction of all kinds of supplementary characters – a Dandy Lover, sprites, shopkeepers, policemen, and so on. There was no real plot, but lots of chases, acrobatic dancing, leaping through windows and popping up through traps. Harlequin had a magic bat with which he effected extraordinary 'trick' changes of props and scenery, often involving punning allusions or social satire: for instance a smart barouche driven by a Dandy was transformed into a farm cart driven by a dirty old carter, or a roulette wheel was transformed into a treadmill in 1822 (some gaming house keepers had been sentenced to the treadmill in prison that year).

In the second half of the nineteenth century the Harlequinade began to decline in importance and the Opening flourished under the influence of the extravaganzas and burlesques of which the mid-Victorians were so fond. Inspired by the wit of writers like W. S. Gilbert, James Planché and H. J. Byron, lesser dramatists turned out hundreds of pantomimes annually, packed with puns and topical jokes. Here are a couple of the more quotable examples from E. L. Blanchard's *Little King Pippin, or Harlequin*

Fortunatus and the Magic Purse, the Drury Lane pantomime of 1865:

'I had an *income,* but at one fell swoop
I went and spent it like a *nincompoop.*'

'*Father:* On points of etiquette I'm a rigid stickler.
Daughter: But pa –
Father: I am, and on this point, *partick'lar.*'

Doggerel of this kind received a welcome transfusion of fresh blood in the shape of an invasion of music hall performers towards the end of the century. It was now that pantomime took the form that is still, by and large, familiar today as a Christmas entertainment, specially for children, with a male Dame and a female Principal Boy. The transvestite tradition in the theatre is a very old one, and it is difficult to establish just at what point the pantomime sex-changes were regarded as indispensable, but there is no doubt that the male Dame has provided one of its most effective features in the hands of a line of brilliant performers like Dan Leno, George Robey, and (both happily still performing) George Lacy and Arthur Askey. Now that the true music hall is extinct, pantomime provides the only opportunity to see performers like this in traditional acts in the live theatre. It is important that the Dame should quite clearly be a man, however outrageously resplendent his costumes; the recent popularity of 'drag' acts is a different line of country entirely.

In *Cinderella* the Dame element is often provided by one or other (or both) of the Ugly Sisters.

Similarly, the Principal Boy is clearly a girl, but a different kind of girl to the Principal Girl; she should have a more brassy voice, a more roguish manner, and, of course, shapely legs. The heroes of fairy stories tend to be somewhat cardboard characters with little personalities of their own, and a good Principal Boy can give a unique dimension to her part. Dorothy Ward is remembered by many people as this century's outstanding performer, though there will be many theatregoers of an older generation who would nominate Clarice Mayne. There has been a tendency in recent years, especially in London, to discard female Principal Boys and not many contemporary actresses understand how to play the part, but any one who has seen Patricia Burke or who can see Pat Kirkwood in it today will understand the magic that can belong to it.

And what of the future? As always, many people criticize pantomime today. 'It is not suitable for children.' But it never was intended *only* for children; it always has been essentially a family entertainment for everyone from grandparents down. 'It spoils the story.' But the story never has been more than a thread on which to hang a kind of variety entertainment. 'It is so vulgar.' Well, some performers are more vulgar than others and some productions have no 'blue' jokes at all, but an element of honest vulgarity is fairly basic in any kind of popular theatre, and pantomime is *popular* theatre at its most elemental, and just about the only kind left in England.

Pantomime today can be criticized on many grounds: the 'books' are banal, the staging is sometimes tatty, they are inadequately rehearsed and poorly directed. The television comics and pop stars who are now so often given star parts may be welcomed as indicating the ability of pantomime to absorb every fresh trend in popular taste, but they sometimes fail to understand the technique of acting in a big theatre and often merely repeat their normal turn without attempting to do it within their roles and in the structure of the story. These faults are less evident in the smaller repertory theatre pantomimes, which I personally find the most enjoyable.

Yet, with all its faults, pantomime is not dying. What has it got that keeps it alive? The answer can only be: a bit of everything. A fairy story for the children, music hall jokes for their parents, slapstick for everyone, circus turns, pretty scenery, dancing and songs, and a chance for everyone to join in a traditional, seasonal, family, ritual rite. Many earnest workers in the theatre today are labouring to create a true popular theatre – in the streets, off-off-Broadway, in cellars and pubs and the fringe of festivals. But such a theatre already exists, almost unnoticed, beneath our noses – traditional, embracing all the performing arts, partly extempore, with audience participation, loved and flocked to by the people. Let us learn from it and support it – the Christmas pantomime.

Above: Twiggy as Cinderella in the 1975 pantomine at the London Casino,
with Roy Kinnear and Hugh Paddick as the Ugly Sisters, Valeria and Cornucopia. On the two following pages are reproduced sheets of characters in
pantomimes adapted for the toy theatre, published in 1854 and 1879.

WEBB'S
Characters & Scenes
IN
HARLEQUIN DAME CRUMP
& THE SILVER PENNY
In 8 Plates of Characters 12 Scenes 1 Plate
of Tricks 1 Transparency & 3 Plates of Wings

Blusterous

With a Book

adapted only to the above

Dame Crump

Pantaloon

Fairy

Blusterous & Fizgig
Printed & Pub by W.WEBB 149 Old Str St Lukes London

Fairy

Clown

WEBB'S NEW DEMONS.

PUBLISHED Nov 3rd 1879 by W. Webb. 146 Old Street. St Lukes. LONDON.

London, Published by B. Pollock. 73, Hoxton Street, Hoxton

Giant Blunderbore with Villagers.

Indian Juggler.

Fig 1.

Giant Blunderbore with Villagers.

Jack.

Dazzelbright.

POLLOCK'S CHARACTERS IN JACK THE GIANT KILLER. *Plate 5.*

Gaffer Strongback.

Clown.

Jack.

Rathksel Hobbinol, the Dukes Esquire.

Jack.

London. Published by B. Pollock. 73, Hoxton Street. Hoxton.

Haymakers.

Villagers.

Jack.

Fig 1.

Above, on the left, the legendary Dan Leno as the Dame in *Mother Goose*, 1902, and below him the still-performing George Lacy, as the Dame in *Mother Goose*, 1936. On the right, Patricia Burke as Prince Charming in *Cinderella* at the London Coliseum in 1939.

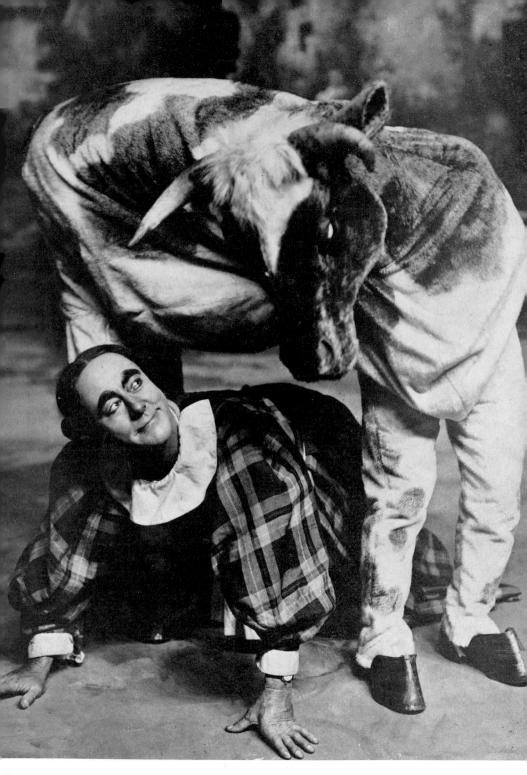

George Robey as the Dame and the Penders as the Cow in *Jack and the Beanstalk* at the London Hippodrome in 1921. (Photographs on this and the opposite page are from the Mander & Mitchenson Theatre Collection.)

MONS. LOUIS AS CLOWN.

London Published by J. REDINGTON 78 Hoxton Street, Formerly called 208 Hoxton Old Town.

44

The Clown was established as the chief comic character in the
harlequinade by Grimaldi, and he had many successors.

PANTALOON

London Published by J. REDINGTON 73 Hoxton Street Formerly called 208 Hoxton Old Town

Pantaloon, shown here in a theatrical print of about 1850,
links pantomime with its origins in the Commedia dell'Arte.

La Vie Parisienne

BY ANTONY D. HIPPISLEY COXE

O N SATURDAY, January 3, 1863, a new French magazine made its début: *La Vie Parisienne*. Round about the same time, after seeing Rigolboche dance the can-can at the Salon Cadet, Jacques Offenbach sat down and wrote his *opéra bouffe* of the same name. This was not merely coincidence. Ludovic Halévy, joint author of the opera's libretto, became a regular contributor to the magazine. But there is a more deeply rooted link. The can-can, that gay, frothy, provocative, agile and ecstatic dance, with its black-stockinged legs saluting one out of a nest of *frous-frous*, was as typical of the French capital under the Second Empire as was the magazine. It is true that the dance originated on the lower rungs of the social ladder while the periodical drew its inspiration from the top; nevertheless, the same naughty gaiety, presented with stylish *élan*, permeated both.

Above: a drawing by Leonnec
Opposite: a drawing by Fabiano

Continued on page 34

F. Fabiano

LA HARPE PLEUREUSE VA SUCCÉDER AUX GAIS PIPEAUX.

The freedom of line in Georges Barbier's drawing, which appeared in December, 1918, reflects the feeling of liberation that followed the First World War. Cupid was a frequent companion to the ladies of *La Vie Parisienne*.

Buissard's cover for June 13, 1925, is typical of the mid twenties, yet the lettering of the title remained virtually unchanged from the first issue to the last.

Illustrations in the twenties are usually full of movement. This drawing is by Hérouard. He contributed regularly to the magazine from 1905 until 1952, always portraying the same woman, who never grew any older. Like Steinlen, Jacques Nam and many others he frequently introduced a cat into the composition.

Bathing and beach scenes were annual subjects for illustrations throughout the magazine's long life. This forceful composition by Vald'Es has the strength of a poster, but,
at the same time it brings out the decorative quality which became so important during
the twenties.

Samedi 19 Avril 1930
68ᵉ ANNÉE N°16 — PRIX: 3 fr. 00

LA VIE PARISIENNE

— VACANCES DE PÂQUES —

The sense of freedom and of movement continued into the 1930's. A good example is this cover by Léonnec, who also maintains the tradition of introducing Cupid, this time as the liberator.

LA VIE PARISIENNE

The change of mood which Mario depicts in this cover is not an innovation but a contemporary expression of an earlier theme; and the lettering of *La Vie Parisienne* remains constant to Marcelin.

LA VIE PARISIENNE

PAR

MARCELIN

MŒURS ÉLÉGANTES
CHOSES DU JOUR-FANTAISIES-VOYAGES
THÉÂTRES-MUSIQUE
MODES

1ʳᵉ ANNÉE·1863

BUREAUX : PLACE DE LA BOURSE, 9

TOUS LES SAMEDIS UN NUMÉRO DE 16 PAGES
Un an, 24 fr. — Six mois, 13 fr. — Trois mois, 7 fr.

Title-page of the first volume, 1863
Opposite: drawing by Raphaël Kirschner

THE FOUNDER of *La Vie Parisienne* was Emil Marcelin Isidore Planat, a thirty-three-year-old illustrator, who also designed its first cover. This, with *Punch*-like consistency, remained unaltered for forty years, and then was only changed by up-dating the clothes in the twelve drawings that surrounded the title.

This read: *La Vie Parisienne, par Marcelin – Mœurs Elégantes – Choses du Jour – Fantaisies – Voyages – Théâtres – Musique – Modes.* The illustrations depicted gentlemen, accompanied by ladies of one sort or another, indulging in elegant pursuits: watching the races, holding forth in the drawing-room, chatting behind the scenes at the Opéra, skating in the Bois de Boulogne.

It was, and remained for most of its life, an *hebdomadaire* – that splendid French word which looks and sounds so much more imposing than a 'weekly' – appearing every Saturday, price 50 centimes, or 24 francs for an annual subscription. Apart from a break caused by World War II it was published regularly, though latterly every month, until the beginning of the present decade.

Marcelin had worked on *Le Journal Amusant*, which also enjoyed a long life, but like *Rabelais*, *La Vie en Rose*, *Le Fêtard* and *La Rigolade*, it was more concerned with humour than amusement. None had the elegance, the style or the cachet of *La Vie Parisienne*, which, as Jacques Sternberg and Pierre Chapelot state in *Un Siècle de PinUp*, was a French precursor of *The New Yorker*, '*assez snob et furieusement Parisien . . . le plus prestigieux bastion de la petite femme, la boîte à délires érotiques. . . .*' (And one cannot possibly translate '*petite femme*' as 'little woman'.)

It never stooped to vulgarity, let alone pornography. It danced with a self-assured elegance and delicate balance a tight-rope more racy than raffish and piquant rather than saucy. It could make its readers smile, even chuckle maybe, but never snigger. A glance could say more than words, but a wink was much too obvious. On occasion its criticism and reviews could mock, but their acidity could never be accused of becoming vitriolic.

From its inception, *La Vie Parisienne* took a particular interest in England. An early number views with a quizzical eye life in a stately English home; Derby Day is featured, and Marcelin even

UNE

JOURNÉE AU CHATEAU

(MŒURS ANGLAISES)

Sans autre compagnie que celle du *Times*.

Voici novembre, et les touristes britanniques, qu'ils appartiennent à l'aristocratique Belgravia ou à Clapham, cette colonie de commerçants, ou à cette vaste région appelée « les Provinces », sont revenus au sein de leurs terres natales et leur climat un peu lourd et épais. Depuis le château ducal, élevant la tête au-dessus des chênes héréditaires, jusqu'au parloir d'épicier ayant pour horizon l'arrière-cour et le tonneau-réservoir, tout Anglais à l'unisson, homme, femme et bébé, se préparent à recevoir les attaques de l'hiver et à rendre leur vie confortable. Le confort est notre Dieu Lares, et nous l'aimons presque autant que l'argent !

Il n'est pas vrai qu'en novembre, nous autres Anglais, nous devenions fous du *spleen* ! Quoique sombres dehors, dans notre intérieur nous sommes gais. Notre nez, extérieurement, est pincé, mais le cœur, soigneusement caché sous nos pardessus, nos fourrures, nos gilets de flanelle et le phlegme britannique, n'en garde que mieux sa chaleur latente. Nos manières, je l'avoue, n'ont rien de cordial. Nous sommes inabordables et *insulaires*; mais le pardessus et la porte une fois pénétrés, nous ne sommes pas de mauvaises gens.

Le *lord lieutenant* du comté, duc, marquis, comte, quel que soit son titre, est « *At home* ».

Pénétrons du regard dans le château de Plantagenista, grand palais féodal au milieu d'un parc qui est presque une forêt, et voyons comment Sa Grâce reçoit ses hôtes.

La cloche du déjeuner a sonné deux fois, et dans la salle à manger, un *gentleman*, habillé pour la chasse, n'a d'autre compagnie que celle du *Times*, qu'il parcourt. Il jette un regard inquiet tantôt sur le couvert mis, tantôt sur l'état du ciel.

Voici que lui arrive l'*honorable Bob Martingale*, son lorgnon, sans lequel on croit qu'il ne peut pas dire ses prières, dans l'œil gauche, et mistress Frontdebœuf et les deux miss Frontdebœuf. La conversation prend le tour le plus vif, et le plus animé :

— *Good morning?* — *Good morning.*
— *Fine day?* — *Charming.* — *Yes!*
— Nous sommes les premiers descendus.

— J'exige toujours qu'on se lève de bonne heure, dit mistress Frontdebœuf, dont les filles sont pleines de sang et de santé, grandes et fortes, mais pas belles.

— Yes, dit l'*honorable Bob*. Bonne chose. — Quoi de nouveau?
— Rien dans le *Times*, dit l'homme au journal.
— *Oh!* — *No!* — *Ah!* — A quelle heure *the meet*? (la chasse) — Onze heures. — C'est que, savez-vous, j'ai un appétit féroce !

L'honorable Bob Martingale, son lorgnon dans l'œil.

A page from an issue of 1863 introducing an account of a visit to an English 'Chateau'

published 'Annie Laurie' under the heading '*Airs Anglais*' (may St Andrew forgive him). The relish with which Edward VII enjoyed his visit to Paris obviously helped to establish a social entente which *La Vie Parisienne* faithfully reflected and maintained through two world wars.

In the 1880s excerpts from Hippolyte Taine's *Survey of English Literature* were published. It may seem strange to find a well-established French philosopher writing for *La Vie Parisienne*, but the man was no less remarkable than the magazine. Although for twenty years he was Professor of Aesthetics and lectured on the history of art at L'Ecole des Beaux Arts, he hardly conformed to the usual academic type. In an early issue his column, 'Notes sur Paris', describes various *Bals Publics*. One of the places he visited was the Casino in the Rue Cadet. Here he describes the girls:

La plus remarquée est Mariette la Toulousaine. Teint bistré, une grosse taille, maigre pourtant, mais tout muscles. Elle lève sa jambe au-dessus de la tête, elle a des caleçons. Elle sue, elle s'éponge, elle fait des efforts comme un sauteur de corde. . . . Elle parle et ne manque pas de verve, mais les choses qu'elle dit ne peuvent pas s'écrire. Elle danse en relevant ses jupons a pleine poignée. J'ai dit qu'elle avait des caleçons, mais j'ai besoin de le redire.

His contributions to *La Vie Parisienne* subsequently appeared as a book: *La Vie et Opinions de M. Fréderic-Thomas Graindorge, Docteur en Philosophie de l'Université d'Iéna, Principal Associé Commanditaire de la Maison Graindorge et Cie (Huile et Porc Salé à Cincinnati, USA) recueillies et publiées par H. Taine, son exécuteur testimentaire.*

The list of authors who contributed to *La Vie Parisienne* is remarkable: Jules Claretie, Francisque Sarcey, Gustav Droz, Edmond About. One of Maurice Donnay's best known novels, *Education de Prince*, made its début as a serial on its pages. So did two of Colette's most famous titles: *Chéri* and *Mitsou, ou Comment l'Esprit Vient aux Filles*. That Prince of Gastronomes, Curnonsky (Maurice Sailland), collaborated with the poet P. J. Toulet, author of *Contrerimes*, in writing three novels which were first published in the magazine: *Bréviaire des Courtisanes*, *Le Métier d'Amant*, and *Demi-Veuve*; the first two under the pseudonym Perdiccas; but the last, for some reason, carried only Curnonsky's name. One of the articles he wrote just before his death in 1956 was on Champagne, commissioned by the last editor of *La Vie Parisienne*, my good friend L-R Dauven, who has provided so much material for this short history.

Other contemporary contributors included André de Fouquières, Pierre Bonardi, and Francis Carco and Gérard Bauer, both of the Académie Goncourt.

However impressive the list of authors may appear, it is probably the illustrators who made *La Vie Parisienne* famous.

Marcelin, its progenitor and first editor, was a draughtsman. He invented the double spread of women, often in various stages of undress, illustrating themes such as Bouquets of Flowers, Pleasure of the Beach, even *Nuits Blanches*. In every case each example on the crowded page had a long caption linking the female figure to the theme.

Ferdinand Bac, an intimate friend of the Empress Eugénie, was the great illustrator of the beauties of the Second Empire, but by the 1880s the style of drawing and indeed the subject matter had become much more free and easy. The keynote of the period was the boudoir, and drawings of young women dressing (or undressing), particularly putting on (or taking off) their stockings, became *de rigueur*. Even if they were dressed for a country walk the wind would lightly lift their skirts to show a shapely leg.

Henri Gerbault – one of *La Vie Parisienne*'s most regular contributors for some forty years – was the great exponent of scantily clad girls who, whatever clothes they took off, seemed determined to keep their legs covered in black stockings.

In spite of the provocativeness of his poses and his obvious popularity, I do not consider him as typical of *La Vie Parisienne* because his line lacks subtlety. Compared with a great draughtsman such as Steinlen he seems a little coarse. Steinlen's love of cats as well as women was shared by another popular illustrator, Jacques Nam. But *La Belle Epoque* introduced a flood of new illustrators, particularly when Charles Saglio became editor. He was not a draughtsman as were Marcelin and his successor Henri de Montaut. Nor was he at all the same type as the third editor, Armand Baudouin, whom Maurice Donnay found an affable bourgeois, in strange contrast to '*l'esprit Parisien, mondain, psschutt et v'lan*' of the magazine he produced. Saglio was the son of the famous Egyptologist and brother of the theatre designer Drésa, who designed such splendid stage sets for the Opéra. While working on *Le Petit Journal* he noted the drawings of Charles Hérouard, and, after taking over *La Vie Parisienne*, invited him to contribute. Hérouard, like so many of the magazine's illustrators, became an institution. His first drawing was published in 1904 and the last in 1952. He was frequently accused – with justification – of always

*Lit démodé en thuya et palissandre,
avec rideaux de satinette tabac à bor-
dure noire et jaune. Une vieille gra-
vure représentant une des fresques
des loges de Raphaël, et dessous la
photographie du poète, du musicien
aimé.*

Elle s'est tellement abreuvée de
café le matin, de thé dans la journée, dans la soirée, qu'elle ne peut
arriver à fermer l'œil. Elle dévore
ses vers, ou se les répète par cœur,
quand elle a soufflé sa bougie, ou
se chante *ses* divines mélodies, si
c'est un musicien qu'elle honore en
ce moment de ses faveurs... parce
que hors les artistes... pas d'a-
mour ! Ce n'est plus un lit, c'est
un vallon ou une colline de l'Inde,
elle s'y couche en long, en large,
en travers, quelquefois même met
sa tête au pied et ses jambes sur
les oreillers !

*Lit sévère Henri II, à colonnes et baldaquin
de drap découpé, monté sur trois marches. Un
vieux crucifix d'ivoire sur velours noir, bénitier
d'argent dans le fond du lit avec branche de
buis bénit et chapelets artistiques.*

Elle croyait si bien qu'elle allait dormir !
Elle n'avait pu aller au bout d'un chapitre du
roman qu'elle en est en train de lire. Sa lampe
éteinte, elle s'était endormie immédiatement,
mais immédiatement aussi elle s'était réveillée.
Elle n'avait pas dormi dix minutes ! Qui est-ce
qui connaît quelque chose de plus affreux
que de se réveiller à minuit un quart, quand
on croit avoir fait sa nuit ? Elle a trop chaud,
elle lance toutes ses couvertures à droite, à
gauche ; elle a trop froid, elle prend ses oreillers pour édredons. Elle passera toute sa
nuit à faire ce manège : à se découvrir, à se
recouvrir sans livre, l'ouvrir et le fermer. Quand
elle aura assez du lit, elle se promènera dans
sa chambre et rangera ses armoires.

*Joli lit Louis XVI ancien, assez
étroit, en bois sculpté et panneaux
de brocart bleu ciel et argent, avec
ciel empanaché de plumes d'autruche
blanches. Une jolie indécence mytho-
logique sur le fond du lit.*

Elle ne dort jamais bien quand
elle est toute seule, et elle ne dort
pas mieux quand elle est deux, tant
son lit est étroit, on est tout le
temps serré l'un contre l'autre...
Elle se tourne, se retourne sans
jamais arriver à trouver une position qui lui plaise... La nuit porte
conseils, mais quels conseils ! Elle
prend pour confidente ses oreillers
de plume et leur raconte les jolis
tours de plumages qu'elle médite
à l'adresse de ces messieurs.

*Sans aucun style, anglais,
moderne, en cuivre, mais
énorme, solide et résistant ;
couvre-pieds patchwork de
soie, fait avec tous les petits bouts d'étoffe qu'elle a carottés
à droite et à gauche chez sa modiste, chez ses coutu-
rières. Elle l'a fait avec amour pour s'en couvrir avec lui*

Tellement amoureuse, qu'elle est ravie de ne pas
dormir quand il ne peut pas être à côté d'elle, pour
pouvoir penser à lui. S'excite par des lectures sugges-
tives, et une fois qu'il fait nuit dans son alcove elle
se met à le chercher... Le lit est si grand, que, s'il
mettait la main sur lui, elle ne serait pas trop surprise. Le lendemain, elle aura mauvaise mine, ses
yeux seront battus, mais ça lui est égal, elle a passé
toute la nuit avec lui !

Pauvre petit lit de fer à l'aspect déveinard, la tête et les pieds recouverts d'une imitation de toile de Jouy, fond blanc à personnages roses, couvre-pieds au crochet fait par elle. Une étude d'après elle, par lui, au fond du lit.

Dans la journée, elle est trop occupée pour pouvoir le pleurer matériellement, mais une fois remontée dans sa chambrette, sans s'en douter, elle met en tableau vivant les passages les plus brûlants du quatrième chant de l'Énéide, une fois qu'elle s'est étendue sur son lit. Tous les soirs, elle prend sa correspondance et la relit de la première lettre à la dernière, et une fois le petit paquet remis à sa place elle se les répète par cœur... Après les expansions littéraires, c'est au tour des autres, et elle couvre sa place de baisers. Elle ne veut pas dormir, parce que le réveil est encore plus cruel que l'état de veille.

Lit de famille style Empire, en acajou plein, avec bronzes néo-grecs qu'on avait laissés dans les greniers et fait figurer dans les chambres d'amis pendant plusieurs générations. Couvre-pieds édredon en vieille soie de nuance passée. Rideaux de damas de soie avec passementerie assortie.

Lit légitime s'il en fut; peut-être que s'il était moins rocambole ou 1830 son propriétaire aurait plus de plaisir à s'y trouver. De même qu'on se met à table pour faire venir les invités en retard, elle se met au lit dans l'espoir que cela le fera revenir plus vite du ... cercle. Elle tombe de sommeil, mais elle se dresse sur son séant pour ne pas s'endormir. Elle est jalouse... Elle n'éteindra sa lampe que quand elle l'entendra ouvrir la porte, et elle fera semblant de dormir.

Petit nid capitonné dans lequel elle se pelote avant ou après partie; vieux damas de soie recouvert d'anciennes guipures italiennes. Une madone et un saint Sébastien bien vieux. (École de)... Lampe d'église d'argent suspendue au plafond.

C'est là qu'elle peut seulement rêver comme elle l'aime et comme elle l'entend, dans la chaleur du lit, avec toutes sortes de jolies choses sous les yeux, éclairées par sa petite lampe, une merveille d'orfèvrerie. Elle dresse la liste de tous les hommes qu'elle a aimés, et ils sont quelques-uns... tantôt par année, tantôt par état, cette fois-là elle les classe d'une certaine manière, cette fois-ci par certaines qualités... Elle compte sur ses doigts... Il y en a... Il faut qu'elle les trouve. Elle ne s'endormira pas avant que son petit ou son grand répertoire ne soit mis à jour.

moderne, d'exposition, ayant affroyablement cher, avec pré- vernis Martin, guirlandes comme embrasses des ri- aux Léonard de fond, aussi par le tapissier.

n'est ni l'amour ni le désespoir empêchent de dormir. Elle est tement heureuse; elle a un mobiliers les plus luxueux oit possible de rêver, mais ou des filles ou un fils pour els il faut qu'elle mette la sur des Gould ou des Vander- outes les héritières, tous les rs dont on lui a parlé, qu'on présentés ne font pas son e. Elle connaît quelqu'un qui lt une personne... Elle fera sit peut-être la rencontrer elle ou telle maison... Il n'y ment que la nuit qu'elle a le de penser.

Lit de milieu en poirier ciré, couverture à petits carreaux de soie et guipure, oreillers très élégants à entre-deux et transparents de soie écrue.

Elle n'a même pas eu le courage de se déshabiller complètement... Elle est tombée sur son lit, en rentrant chez elle, pas complètement paff, mais assez émue et excitée. Elle a fait sauter l'un après l'autre ses petits souliers, a dégrafé un bouton ou deux de son corset... Quand elle s'est sentie un peu mieux, s'est déshabillée à la six quatre deux, mais elle entend sonner toutes les heures et il fera grand jour quand, exténuée de s'être étirée toute la nuit, elle pourra fermer l'œil.

drawing the same woman, and he cheerfully pleaded guilty. 'The readers of La Vie Parisienne,' he said, 'have come to expect a certain type. If I were to change my model they would be thrown off beat, become disenchanted. For them, the petite femme of La Vie Parisienne must remain as constant as our signatures.' Readers were always asking the illustrators if such-and-such a drawing was not modelled on so-and-so? Each character became closely identified in the readers' minds with a real person, but it was always either an actress or a fashionable demi-mondaine of the day.

Hérouard's view was presumably shared by Maurice Millière, whose girls were always wide-eyed, crowned by golden curls, and looked exactly like his wife. Brunelleschi, on the other hand, showed his skill not so much in creating a type, but in his remarkable sense of composition. Georges Léonnec excelled at catching the fashions of the day, while Gerda Wegener enjoyed the unique position of being the only woman to draw women for men's delight. Raphaël Kirchner, who came from Austria at the beginning of the century, frequently contributed delicate little drawings of pretty girls against Art Nouveau backgrounds, until the outbreak of World War I.

However, of all the illustrators I find Fabiano the most notable. This Breton, whose real name was Coup, was a fine painter who turned out illustrations merely to make easy money. For this reason his drawings may sometimes appear a little facile, though they are always beautifully composed. One has only to look at his studies of the nude, let alone his canvasses painted in Tahiti, to see how good a draughtsman he was. The girls he created for La Vie Parisienne became so popular that they were christened 'Fabianettes'.

Caricature never played a prominent part in La Vie Parisienne, although Mich produced some delightful coloured sketches, a little reminiscent of Caran d'Ache, and some excellent caricatures by Sem were published in the early years of the century. In 1911 one finds, surprisingly, Sacha Guitry contributing this kind of drawing, but the great scoop of that year was printing the work of Candide, a pseudonym which hid the identity of Jean Cocteau.

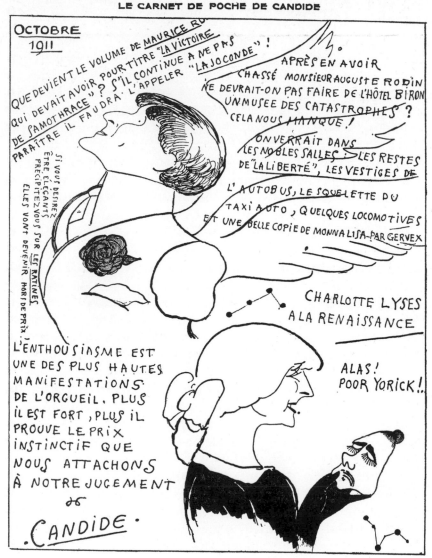

A caricature in an issue of October 1911 by 'Candide', who was Jean Cocteau

Although one may well be surprised by the names one finds amongst the literary and graphic contributors, one cannot help being staggered by the names on the list of readers. In 1905, amongst those who had taken out regular subscriptions were: His Imperial Majesty the Czar Nicholas II, His Imperial Highness the Grand Duke Peter Nicholas, His Imperial Highness the Grand Duke Paul of Russia, His Majesty King Carlos I of Portugal, His

Royal Highness the Prince of Bulgaria, His Majesty King George I of the Hellenes, and His Majesty King Edward VII. It was read in clubs such as White's, Boodles and the St James's in London, and the Jockey and Travellers' in Paris. Nothing remained as delightfully French as *La Vie Parisienne*; so it was natural for all those who loved the good life to buy the magazine with alacrity and read it with avidity. It achieved its greatest popularity in World War I, when its circulation topped 40,000 copies a week, for it brought vividly to those in the trenches, whether they were princes or *poilus*, the life that had been left behind, but to which they hoped to return on their next leave. Editorially *La Vie Parisienne* became war-conscious, not merely providing escapism, but incorporating photographic coverage from the various fronts. A feature which contributed to its growing popularity were the small advertisements inserted by soldiers and sailors seeking 'godmothers' with whom they could correspond. Two, taken at random, read: '*Officier, ayant cafard, demande marraine jeune et jolie*', and '*Deux marins demandent correspondance avec gentilles marraines pour charmer leur longues heures de plongée. Charmantes marraines venez à leur secours et écrivez à J. Duverger et R. Ducaur, Sousmarin Joëssel. BCN.*'

Those who advertised were not solely French. I have heard of a young English subaltern, straight from school in 1918, whose last few months of life were made less lonely because he found, through *La Vie Parisienne*, a girl with whom he could correspond. Less personal advertisements had appeared since the 1870s. In 1883, for instance, No. 49 Rue Jean Jacques Rousseau was advertised for sale at a price of 500,000 francs, and one of the most constant advertisements which used photographs at the turn of the century was for a milliner with the very ungallic name of Lewis.

After the war the magazine continued along its own frothy, frilly and frivolous, yet elegantly urbane way. Art Nouveau was replaced by Art Moderne and Déco; the emancipation of women led to short skirts and long cigarette holders, but the themes of *La Vie Parisienne* remained constant. Girls still adjusted their stockings; the wind still lifted their skirts; and pyjamas could be just as revealing as nightgowns. Cuckolds were still figures of fun, and Love was the eternal refrain.

This was the time when I took to buying *La Vie Parisienne*, not regularly, but maybe four or five times a year. Aged sixteen, I wanted desperately to belong to the twenties, which were almost over, and to be considered sophisticated. Paris was my goal. I was convinced that Montparnasse was more stimulating than Bloomsbury, just as the Rue du Faubourg St Honoré was smarter than Bond Street. Everyone well knew that nowhere else could one find such good food, such exquisite wine, such wanton women . . . And by reading *La Vie Parisienne* – even by just carrying it around – I felt a part of the beautiful world.

Then came World War II, and once again *La Vie Parisienne* set out to appeal to the troops, both English and French, by printing the captions in both languages. But the Second World War was very different from the First. Under the German occupation Paris was neither frivolous nor light-hearted. Life was austere and underground. So *La Vie Parisienne* suspended publication. It was bought by M. Georges Ventillard in 1951, and in 1953 he invited the last in the great dynasty of editors, L-R Dauven, to take it over.

Photographers played an increasingly important part and André Diénès (the favourite photographer of Marilyn Monroe, who was responsible for the famous calendar), Giancarlo Belli and Serge Jacques all regularly contributed. But the illustrators were not forgotten. For most of its life *La Vie Parisienne* had published special albums. Before World War I these had carried titles such as: *Fantaisies Féminins*, *La Chasse d'Amour*, *Le Corps de la Femme* and *Etude de la Toilette*. L-R Dauven concentrated more on the art of the painters than such evocative titles, bringing out a special sixty-page number each year with eight pages of full colour, on the works of G. Detrè, Jean-Gabriel Domergue, Edmond Heuzé and Louis Touchagues. This period was perhaps the second flowering of the magazine, but it was also its swan song. In 1970 Jean-Pierre Ventillard, who had succeeded his father, decided that *La Vie Parisienne* had run its course. It would have been too big a financial risk to keep the magazine going in the hope that fashion would turn full circle. *La Vie Parisienne* belonged to a leisurely era which it reflected with subtlety and grace; its world was the Boulevard, where a *flâneur* could turn slowly to admire a pretty girl and follow her with his eyes. And the girl would know she was being admired without even turning her head, and somehow, imperceptibly it seems, she could let her unknown admirer know that she knew. To appreciate fully the subtleties of life one must have leisure. L-R Dauven says it was the Jet Set that killed the life of the Boulevard. After all, the faster one travels the more obvious the sights must be, and those who run can read nothing smaller than the bold type of a poster. The girlie magazines of today – blatant, stark and full-frontal – are a reflection of the Jet Age. Just as the can-can symbolized the Paris of:

> . . . . lovely ladies, on cushions easy
> Driving down the Champs Elysées

so does strip-tease reflect the jeans and hamburgers at the drug-store counter that one now finds in the shadow of the Arc de Triomphe. Yet Paris, though eternal, is like *les petites femmes de La Vie Parisienne*, constant only in inconstancy, and anything may happen.

In the meantime let *La Vie Parisienne* remind us of an age when a man of the world did not have to dash madly about the face of the earth; and that although sparkle and froth may be evanescent, without them the things one savours, such as champagne – and even beer, come to that – taste pretty flat.

The World
of Jeffery Farnol

BY E. S. TURNER

J EFFERY FARNOL was a brass-founder's son who made a
spanking £40,000 from his first romantic novel, written in a
rat-ridden studio in New York, and published in Britain in
1910. *The Broad Highway* was brash, flamboyant and as honest as
the pound sterling of those days. Reviewing this 'picaresque' tale
in *The Times*, a critic observed that Farnol had 'taken hints' from
Le Sage, Fielding, Smollett and Borrow, but had failed because he
had tried to revive a dead convention. For the next forty years
the author of this triumphant failure exploited the dead convention for all he was worth, turning out such runaway successes
as *The Amateur Gentleman, The Honourable Mr Tawnish, Sir John Dering*
and *Black Bartlemy's Treasure*.

Between the world wars Farnol was a household name, to the
occasional embarrassment of others who bore it. Some authors
are read, others are devoured; and Farnol was devoured with
equal relish by school children and adults. In the main, reviewers
took him no more seriously than he took himself, being content
to throw overboard their critical faculties and cling on for an
exciting ride; yet from time to time, to show their scholarship,
they traced his 'influences' not only to the masters already
mentioned but also to Bunyan, Cervantes, Defoe, Dickens and
Thackeray.

When Jeffery Farnol died in 1952 *The Times* was still wary of over-
praise. His books had 'endeared themselves to a happily more
innocent younger generation than the present'. He had been
'a genuine enough storyteller' in 'a pulsing, youthful way',
wearing his heart on his sleeve but writing with his tongue in his
cheek. Today, Farnol's romances are still in demand at libraries
and quite a few of his forty-odd titles have recently been reprinted. It is likely that his borrowers include a high proportion
of those whom he first captured in youth.

John Jeffery Farnol was born in Birmingham in 1878. When he was about ten the family moved south and lived for some years at Lee, near Lewisham, whence he explored and fell in love with the Kent countryside. According to a memoir by his younger brother Edward, he was a vigorous member of a 'purity squad', consisting of a dozen young fist fighters, who discouraged the louts of Deptford from surrounding girls on the pavement and insulting them (the nineties were naughty at all levels). His mother thought Jeffery had literary talent, but his father sent him to work in a brass foundry in Birmingham. There he had innumerable punch-ups. Eventually (or so his book jackets used to proclaim) he was sacked for knocking down a foreman who called him a liar. It is hard to believe that he was never the one to give offence.

At twenty, without bothering to tell his parents of his plans, Farnol married an American girl. Then, in 1902, after quarrelling with his father, he went with his wife to America, where he quarrelled with his father-in-law. He was selling a few short stories, but found it necessary to work for two years as a scene painter for the Astor Theatre, New York. At night, homesick in the theatre's squalid studio, he wrote *The Broad Highway*. Two American publishers rejected it outright; a third pronounced it 'too long and too English'. An actor friend of Farnol offered to show the manuscript to a Boston publisher, but 'forgot' to do so, and it was eventually recovered from the bottom of his trunk. In some disgust Farnol sent it to his wife to destroy (something he could surely have done for himself); instead, she packed it off to a family friend in England, Shirley Byron Jevons, then editor of *The Sportsman*. The enthusiastic Jevons kindled the interest of Sampson, Low and Marston, who sought the opinion of the author-critic Clement K. Shorter, chiefly because he was an authority on George Borrow. Shorter's opinion was more than favourable. After a slow start, the book went like a hurricane, but had the staying power that a hurricane lacks; by 1914 it had sold about 600,000 copies. The American rights were bought by the Boston firm on which the absent-minded actor had failed to call; and a high proportion of the profits came from the country where it had been judged 'too English'.

The basic idea of *The Broad Highway*, which is set, like so many of Farnol's novels, in Regency England, may well have been borrowed from George Borrow; but there was a flourishing 'open road' cult to which Stevenson, Whitman, Bliss Carman and many others had contributed. 'I felt some desire,' says Lavengro, 'to meet with one of those adventures which, upon the roads of England, are as plentiful as blackberries in autumn.' In *The Broad Highway* these sentiments are echoed by the well-born scholar-adventurer, Peter Vibart, who takes to the road to study Man and find high adventure.

This book, like Farnol's others, shows the same love of fisticuffs that marks *Lavengro*, and something too of distaste for over-refined society. If it is picaresque, at least the leading picaroon is vastly more virtuous than his literary predecessors. Strictly, such a novel needs no plot, relying for excitements on chance encounters; but Farnol, though much indebted to 'hedge taverns' and strange wayfarers, encompasses his tales within the favourite nineteenth-century plot; that is, there is always a great inheritance to be earned, fought for, or restored to the rightful heir. It was the plot for which millions had an inextinguishable affection, and Farnol was not one to deprive them of it.

In *The Broad Highway*, before Peter Vibart sets off to see the world on ten guineas, he rejects the terms of an uncle's will under which £500,000 will be payable either to himself or to his rascally cousin, Sir Maurice, depending on which of them woos and wins the reigning toast, Lady Sophia Sefton. Priggish Peter shrinks from the idea of marrying some trull whose name is on everybody's lips, and who is credited with having ridden her horse up the steps of St Paul's and down again. Hardly has he set off before he is robbed of his ten guineas; then, in quick time, he challenges a champion pugilist, watches a fatal duel, is shot at by a madman and rescues an oppressed lady (spurning a Daemon who urges him to kiss her in a dark wood). The broad highway turns out to be peopled, even infested, with literary tinkers, one-legged heroes, Scots fiddlers, garrulous Ancients, preachers and epileptics. In due course Peter becomes a village blacksmith, a trade much esteemed by the author, perhaps as a result of having worked in a foundry.

Since old Tubal Cain first taught man how to work in brass and iron, who ever heard of a sneaking, mean-spirited, cowardly blacksmith? To find such a one were as hard a matter as to discover the Fourth Dimension, or the carcass of a dead donkey.

Farnol's blacksmiths tend to be men who did well at Trafalgar or Waterloo, which is more than can be said for his footmen and moneylenders.

It is while clouting the anvil that Peter succours another mettlesome lady, improbably calling herself Charmian Brown. To shield her from molestation it is necessary to give her a room in his cottage; an arrangement which, since there is no question of a chaperone, he would have censured most strongly had it been proposed by any other man in England. Indeed, no other man in England would have believed in the innocence of his motives. In case he is again tempted by Daemons, he hands Charmian a sharp knife to use against anyone who enters her bedroom. A man of high standards expects equally high standards in his women. When Peter finds that Charmian has been meeting an unexplained stranger he accuses her of being 'a Messalina, a Julia, a Joan of Naples – beautiful as they, and as wanton'. The lady does not care for such talk from a classically educated black-smith, rescuer though he may be. Who is Charmian, anyway? The reader will readily guess, but Peter, despite all the clues, has to be told. Farnol heroes are not very quick on the uptake.

Indeed, the Farnol hero, that one-man purity squad, is a fairly rum case (Peter Vibart differs from the others only in his ability to bandy Epictetus with wayfarers). Half-champ, half-chump, the brawny paladin despises fancy manners and conversation. Like his creator, he is a shade over-ready to let fly with the 'naked mauleys'. Friendship between males is scarcely valid until the two parties have knocked each other dizzy, or 'tapped the claret'. It is probably the Borrow influence again: 'There's the wind on the heath, brother; if I could only feel that I would gladly live for ever. . . . We'll now go to the tents and put on the gloves, and I'll try to make you feel what a sweet thing it is to be alive, brother.' In *The High Adventure* Jeremy says to an exhausted aristocrat, 'My dear fellow, you need fresh air, exercise and a friend to pummel you heartily.' Jeremy also has a near-concussive bout with Jessamy Todd, a prize-fighter who, having killed an adversary, has turned to God. There are no hard feelings, rather the reverse:

Clasping sudden arms about the ex-champion, Jeremy squeezed him impulsively and mightily; whereupon Jessamy squeezed back and flushed immediately and stared up at the blue heaven, while Jeremy scowled down at the sparkling water again, and both sat mumchance like the very Britons they were.

If it comes to a rough-and-tumble against a gang of villains, there is another permitted weapon besides naked mauleys. 'My lads, good fellows all,' cries a character in *Murder by Nail*, 'I want no murderous steel or pistol work. Trust to honest sticks.' In *Heritage Perilous* the hero, forced reluctantly into a duel, chooses honest cutlasses (and severs his opponent's right hand).

As a lover, the Farnol hero is a dire blunderer. Having put the high-born damsel in his debt, he loses no time in rubbing her the wrong way. The dialogue is mostly sparring and recrimination; but who would wish pages of endearments? Women are hard put to civilize these surly, possessive, mumchance fellows who hate to see them speaking a civil word to anyone else. In the main, Farnol heroines are assembled in a Photofit manner: their throats are soft creamy columns, their chins have fugitive dimples, their lips are scarlet, their nostrils delicate, their voices contralto, their fingers slim and imperious; they are light of foot and, though God-fearing, they are not above sly bewitchments. Constitutionally, despite slim waists, they are astonishingly robust; for when their rescuers find them swept ashore half-drowned they are required to dry their clothes on their persons. Any other proposal would bring a 'warm, crimson tide' to the cheeks of both parties. In *Black Bartlemy's Treasure* Lady Joan Brandon, aged twenty-six, and Martin Conisby, aged twenty-seven, both in full possession of their faculties, spend upwards of two months sleeping platonically beside a camp fire on a Caribbean isle, addressing each other as 'Comrade'. Inhibiting their relationship is Conisby's consuming desire for vengeance on those of Lady Joan's family who made him a galley slave; she will not give her heart to one obsessed by such an evil passion.

One day, however, Martin is carried away, 'pinning her arms in a cruel embrace' and kissing her until 'sun and trees and green grass seemed to spin and whirl dizzily'. The lady will for ever remember this as the night 'the beast broke loose'. Her rebuke is as follows: 'Where hate is, true love can never be, and love howsoever vehement is gentle and reverent, and, being of God, a very holy thing! But you have made it a thing of passion, merciless and cruel – 'tis love debased.' The shamed Martin withdraws to another part of the island so that she may sleep safe from one beast at least; but he leaves her a gun to discharge in emergency. It does not stay long undischarged.

Farnol's second big success was *The Amateur Gentleman*, in which he turned round the idea of his first book. Barnabas, son of a prize-fighting innkeeper, inherits £700,000 and sets off to London ('Oho for youth and life and the joy of it!') to storm the polite world, only to be disgraced for his humble origins. He is the first, but not the last, hero to be saddled with the task of reclaiming the fair one's wastrel brother; a delicate business, because if he pays off the debts he risks being accused of trying to buy the lady. *The Amateur Gentleman* introduces that curious detective Jasper Shrig, the iron-hatted Bow Street Runner. 'Vell, sir, I'm vot they call a bashaw of the pigs,' says Shrig, who is Dickensian in name and speech. His duty is to 'circumwent and conflummerate' by any means 'Wiciousness' and 'Windictiveness'. As a youth he was 'a champion buzman . . . a prime rook at queering the gulls', but he now lives only to keep the gallows tree well draped with rogues. His official terms of reference are not stated. He just wanders the country entering in his little book the names of those whose faces stamp them as Capital Coves; and then, in tabular form, he notes date when spotted, date on which the coves commit murder and date of execution. He is capable of playing Gothic tricks with skulls, in order to trap those with bad consciences. From time to time he recruits to his service urchins whose wits have been sharpened by living rough, as did many other fictional sleuths, notably Sexton Blake. How the handful of detectives on the strength of the Bow Street Runners really operated is knowledge not to be gained from the pages of Farnol.

From time to time Farnol strayed into the Middle Ages, as in

Beltane The Smith and *The Geste of Duke Jocelyn*. Two seventeenth-
century stories are *Black Bartlemy's Treasure* and *Martin Conisby's
Vengeance*; for these pirate tales, he seems to have 'taken hints'
from Bunyan rather than Borrow ('Who art thou,' cries Flesh,
'to adventure things so great and above thy puny strength to
perform? Who art thou?' 'I am God!' answers Man-soul, 'since
finite man am I only by reason of thee, base, coward Flesh.')
In *Over The Hill* Farnol turned to the 1715 Rebellion.

Like so many romantic novelists, Farnol was happiest in the
Regency of bucks and bruisers. It is necessary to say, however,
that one can learn more about the Regency from a single newspaper of 1815 than from the whole corpus of Farnol. We hear
nothing of Luddites, peasant unrest, Reform agitation, child
slavery; we simply get costumed derring-do in the traditional
romantic setting. As for Farnol's Kent, so often featured, it could
as easily be Sussex or Shropshire. It is an idealized, idyllic land,
bird-haunted, with ringing hammers, taverns with glorious
kitchens, dogs which growl instinctively at villains, and glorious,
hospitable aunts who believe in subordination and the gallows.

Popular romance calls inexorably for an inflated way of speech.
Farnol's works have their share of tushery and fustian; the wind
on the heath could be the wind of flatulence. 'Almost every
speech begins with Ay, Yea, Nay, Ha, Ho, Aha, Oho or Verily',
noted a critic of *The King Liveth*. Another reviewing tease was to
illustrate the author's monstrous piling up of adjectives. Thus,
a single page of *Murder By Nail* will yield slimy, haunting, nerve-
racking, ghastly, brutal, awful, terrible, merciless, despairing,
frightful, blinding, remorseless, rank, black, fetid, appalling,
noisome, whimpering, shuddering, breathless, sickening, despairing, passionate and fearful (twice); among nouns, terror,
despair, loathing, torment, maniac, frenzy, corruption, loath-
someness, swoon, horror and Death-in-Life; and among verbs,
overwhelmed, prisoned, dreaded, wounded, writhed, nauseate
and stupefy. When possible, Farnol would work in archaic
words like mumchance, hugeous, baresark (for berserk), day-
spring, trixy (for tricksy?) and maugre (for despite). He awarded
capital letters lavishly, to Flesh, Sin, Ignorance, Circumstance
and the Essential Feminine. His characters passed from the

Valley of Dreadful Night over the Hill of Blessed Hope into the Land of Heart's Delight. He never funked an accent or a style of speech; his pages are a treasure-house of Egad, Damme, Zounds, Hist, Losh, Hoot-toot, Indade, Bad Cess, Haw, Yassuh, Yah-Boo, Avast, Sink Me, Mark'ee, Pish, *Tiens, Pardieu, Sapristi* and a score of other old favourites. Women are 'the sex' and married men are Benedicts. In common with his eighteenth-century predecessors Farnol was addicted to chapter headings like 'Of Storm, and Tempest, and of the Coming of Charmian' and 'Of an Ethical Discussion which the Reader is Advised to Skip'.

There was a bare-faced innocence, and even impudence, about the world of Jeffery Farnol, which was as artificial as the world of Wodehouse. He existed to entertain, not to teach history by stealth. He loved lovers. Romance was virtually all, and its conventions, shamelessly invoked, enabled him to get away with preposterous situations; though undoubtedly his gusto and buoyancy as a storyteller, his mastery of plot and counter-plot, his springing of constant surprises all helped to prevent the reader from querying what was going on. There was no message, other than that manliness and honesty are to be admired. Some will say he helped to constrain the Englishman's love-making, confirming him in his tendency to put women on pedestals or pinnacles; but that reproach must be spread over a great many of his contemporaries. Possibly he helped to make English girls more patient with brawny clods.

Farnol's early books are generally regarded as his best, despite a certain self-indulgence which passed for philosophy. He enjoyed his success, entertaining his fellow writers and wintering in Italy, but quarrelling, alas, with his younger brother. His last book, *Justice by Midnight*, was completed after his death by his second wife. The basic secret of his triumph was set out, simply but adequately, by Clement Shorter, writing in 1915: 'The great reading public of any age will not be bullied into reading the authors who have reached the dignity of classics. The writer who can catch some element of the spirit of the "masters" and modernize it is destined to win the favour of the crowd. And thus Mr Jeffery Farnol has entered into his kingdom.'

Pop Poems BY J. J. CURLE

'SOMETHING IN THE CITY'

I GO WALKING through the City
Where nobody walks but me;
On a Sunday I can have that
World of money all for free.
There's a vast and empty silence
Round the death of Bulls and Bears,
Like a jungle that's relented
– Dedicated to fair shares.

The Exchange exchanges kisses
And the Stock walks on the street;
Ticker-tape is my confetti
And the Mint is for my meat.
It is like an empty stage, where
Life's just goin' to begin,
As I walk there Sunday morning
With a world of love to win.

She lives down there in the City
Where nobody walks but me;
She grows, in that twisted kingdom,
Straight and graceful as a tree,
– And on Sunday, when I visit,
Wealth is nothin'; power is dumb,
As I pass – where greed is humbled –
To my taste of Kingdom Come.

The Exchange exchanges kisses
And the Stock walks on the Street;
Ticker-tape is my confetti
And the Mint is for my meat.
It is like an empty stage, where
Life's just goin' tobegin,
As I walk there Sunday morning
With a world of love to win.

ANSWER!

HE IS THE fab-u-lousiest man I've ever met;
    He turns me on and off just like a tap all day;
    He never even seems to look at me, and yet
Wherev'r I turn up he's somewhere in my way.

> *How can I know what he's thinking,*
> *When he never lets me see*
> *In behind that never-blinking*
> *Look he never turns on me?*
> *I must know. I'm so uncertain;*
> *All my love could turn to hate*
> *If he cannot lift that curtain.*
> *– How long have we got to wait?*

I find him looking past my shoulder in the crowd;
I find him always going my way – but not with me.
Are both of us that much too humble or too proud?
Is he indiff'rent or is he in love with me?

> *How can I know what he's thinking . . .*

He is the damna-bless'dest man I've ever known.
I feel I'd like to strike him dead, but when I try
To cut his roots out of my life, I have to own
That if I cut that deep I think that I should die.

> *How can I know what he's thinking,*
> *When he never lets me see*
> *In behind that never-blinking*
> *Look he never turns on me?*
> *I must know. I'm so uncertain;*
> *All my love could turn to hate*
> *If he cannot lift that curtain.*
> *– How long have we got to wait?*

JUST FOR MY SAKE

WAKING in the morning;
　Turning, stretching, yawning;
　Looking on the pillow next to mine.
Knowing it's your head
Beside mine in the bed,
I – feel so fine.
I – feel – so – fine.

– But, as I bend to kiss you,
I almost want to cry;
– Got such a sudden wish to keep
You just that way you lie.
Though time is sliding past us
And soon you're bound to wake,
Sleep on another moment
For my sake . . . just for my sake.

Leaves upon the ceiling
Share my happy feeling,
Spun there by the sunlight through the trees.
Lock of hair that lies
Warm over mouth and eyes
Stirs – with life's breeze;
Stirs – with – life's – breeze.

But, as I bend to kiss you . . .

Waking in the morning;
Turning, stretching, yawning;
Looking on the pillow next to mine.
Knowing it's your head
Beside mine in the bed,
I – feel so fine.
I – feel – so – fine.

– But as I bend to kiss you . . .

EASY STREET

DAD STOPPED work last Friday
    At the fact'ry gate:
    Thirty-eight years steady
– Hardly ever late;
Smiled at ev'rybody,
Wasn't paid too well.
Mates said 'why not fight it?'
Dad said 'what the hell!'

Nothing's going to alter now,
Nothing's going to change:
Death has drawn a bead on him,
– Only needs the range.

Got no golden handshake,
No subscription gift;
Just the street before him
When he quit the shift:
Has to sell the pigeons,
Drop the Christmas club,
Scared of meeting friends, he
Can't treat in the pub.

Nothing's going to alter now . . .

Got no taste for reading,
– Too late to begin;
Plays the pools by habit,
– Knows he'll never win;
Feels his muscles slacken;
No one stops to talk:
Sometimes does the shops, 'cos
That will make a walk.

Nothing's going to alter now . . .

You can give him money;
You can't give him life.
– It's the cutting edge, that
Justifies the knife.
Watch him sitting pretty
– Ev'ry need supplied –,
Till the day you find he's
Quit on *you* and died.

Nothing's going to alter now,
Nothing's going to change;
Death has drawn a bead on him,
– Only needs the range.

FIRE GONE UP IN SMOKE

ID YOU ever love me;
   Can one ever know?
   Did I ever please you;
Was that all a show?
What is it you've taken?
Can I ever tell;
Is it just our future
Or my past as well?

I thought living easy;
All we did seemed fun.
Was it ever real, love;
How warm was that sun?
What you've left behind you
Is a blank in me.
I thought you were there, love.
– Could I really see?

When you said, 'It's ended',
That was no more true
Than the things you whispered
Once when love was new.
Are we diff'rent people;
Have we altered so?
I'm forced to remember.
– Shall I ever know?

I thought living easy . . .

Where can I go back to?
Where begin again?
What have I to build on
That will bear the strain?
You were my foundation;
When you moved, I broke.
What have I to live for
– Fire gone up in smoke?

I thought living easy . . .

ONCE

WALKING DOWN the street, where
Once we used to walk;
Pausin' at the seat, where
Once we'd sit and talk,
– Ev'rything seems altered
– Am I altered too? –
Was it *I* who walked here,
Walked and talked with *you*?

Once the words came out so easy,
Once we had so much to say,
Once it seemed we'd hardly get it
All into four hours a day.
Love, I can't go on much longer;
Is that thing we were quite dead?
Have you not a single word, to
Bring back life to all we've said?

We still walk together.
– Folk who ought to know
Think we *are* together
– Fooled by what we show.
But the silence lengthens.
On that seat where we
Talked, I talk – but never
Hear you answer me.

Once the words came out so easy . . .

Shoulder brushing shoulder
As we stroll along,
People never dream that
Anything is wrong.
I walk with a stranger
Never speaks to me,
– Looking for that couple
We once used to be.

Once the words came out so easy,
Once we had so much to say,
Once it seemed we'd hardly get it
All into four hours a day.
Love, I can't go on much longer;
Is that thing we were quite dead?
Have you not a single word, to
Bring back life to all we've said?

PARTING

L AY YOUR HEAD upon my shoulder;
    Wrap my coat around your arm;
    We'll get warm as night gets colder;
Nothing hurt and nothing harm.

Here upon a bench together,
Waiting for the cruel train;
Nothing to discuss but whether
We shall ever meet again.
We're so good for one another,
But it isn't going to be.
We would choke and we would smother.
– How it hurts, love, to be free.

Take my hand in gentle fingers;
Smooth my hair the way you do.
How the wonder of it lingers
That I had to fall for *you.*

Here upon a bench together . . .

When we part and all is ended,
We shall never quite forget.
Since least said is quickest mended,
Best say nothing, love, – and yet!

Here upon a bench together,
Waiting for the cruel train;
Nothing to discuss but whether
We shall ever meet again.
We're so good for one another,
But it isn't going to be.
We would choke and we would smother.
– How it hurts, love, to be free.

Books
that Come to Life

BY IONA & PETER OPIE

WITH PHOTOGRAPHS BY
DERRICK WITTY

NOBODY buys a book that is just ordinary. Publishers rely for their sales on the acknowledged usefulness of their publications, or on the fame of their authors, or on the skill of their illustrators, or on the sumptuousness of their productions, or on their relative cheapness, or – as in the case of *The Saturday Book* doubtless – on their having all these attributes at once. But what of the publisher with no vital information to impart, with only hack writers and stylized illustrators in his employ, and with only average means of production? For a surprisingly long time now there have been firms, large and small, particularly firms catering for the young, who have sought to put life into their books by the crudest of all possible means, by representing life mechanically. Their artists may not be able to depict movement, so the figures in their pictures are made to move in reality; they may not be able to convey the illusion of depth, so they produce pictures that are actually three-dimensional; they may be incapable of portraying a cow mooing, so a mooing noise is in fact contrived. Their argument seems to be that if a book is shaped like a puffer-train, and has a couple of revolving wheels at the bottom, even a two-year-old will appreciate it is a piece of railwayana. And, before we know where we are, the non-readers amongst us, who seemingly include the majority of visitors to antique supermarkets and buyers at Sotheby's children's-book sales, are valuing these non-books above real books, and paying for them as if they contained the gems of our literary heritage.

The fun in these books – and fun there undoubtedly is – is

however not difficult to identify. It lies in their ability to surprise, as when we open a commonplace-seeming *carte-de-visite* album and unwittingly trigger off a musical box buried in its depths. This point, however, needs emphasizing: mechanical books should look like ordinary books. Their success is to be measured by the ingenuity with which their bookish format conceals unbookish characteristics. Nister's *The Land of Long Ago* is no more than half an inch thick when closed, but contains three-dimensional scenes with a combined depth of three and a half feet. Bookano Books, of the late 1930s, utilize the opening of the book not merely to make cut-out figures pop up but to become active: the part-shutting and re-opening of the book enables gnomes to keep sawing logs, and birds to keep flapping their wings, without any recourse to levers.

Who first invented a mechanical device in a book we do not pretend to know. In the *Astronomicum Caesareum* of Petrus Apianus, published at Ingolstadt in 1540, is an assemblage of coloured movable parts with which the position of Mars can be determined at any given time. In Jacques Bassantin's *Astronomique discours*, printed at Lyons in 1557, an intricate circular diagram with moving parts is provided '*pour trouuer le vray lieu de Venus au Zodiaque*'. And in Gallucci's *Coelestium Corporum*, produced in Venice in 1603, no fewer than fifty-one diagrams are to be found with volvelles and movable pointers, an abundance that puts to shame some present-day novelty books.

These volvelles and pointers were, of course, for scientific use; as were, supposedly, the layer upon layer of coloured cut-out flaps in the books containing 'anatomical models' so popular with the curious at the beginning of the present century. In the early days books with moving parts that were for diversion rather than information were uncommon, though the 'lotteries' and revolving 'indexes', with which a reader might know his character in George Wither's *Collection of Emblemes*, 1635, scarcely advanced the cause of science; and the gimmick was imitated, indeed reproduced, by Nathaniel Crouch in *Delights for the Ingenious*, 1684.

The great advances in book illustration in the eighteenth century made it inevitable, perhaps, that some publisher, whose engravers were not of the top rank, should employ craft rather than art to attract attention. In 1766 or 1767 Robert Sayer in Fleet Street produced the first of a series of booklets in which two flaps were hinged to each page, one downwards from the top, the other upwards from the bottom, and of such a size that they met neatly in the middle to form a single picture. When the poetical description had been studied, the reader lifted the top or bottom flap, as directed, which instantly revealed, with no change of location, the next action in the story; and when the second flap was lifted a subsequent action was exposed, which sometimes brought about a complete metamorphosis in the characters. During the next half century at least six publishers issued these 'turn-up' books or 'harliquinades'; and books using the same principle continue, in fact, to be manufactured to this day.

What is curious is that even when these turn-up books appeared on the market two hundred years ago they were not new. We ourselves possess a home-made one, fashioned on precisely the same plan, in which – amongst the transformations – Adam turns into a mermaid; and this homely amusement was given to a child in 1741. Further, the tradition there certainly was in the eighteenth century for the private manufacture of turn-up books seems to go back to the middle of the seventeenth century. In the British Museum we find a work entitled *The Beginning, Progress and End of Man*, printed in London by B. Alsop, for T. Dunster, 1650; and the flaps, the subject-matter, and the opening verses of our manuscript metamorphosis are all but identical to those of the seventeenth-century example.

To the connoisseur, the golden age of the mechanical book was the second half of the nineteenth century. If the claim made by Dean and Son in the 1860s is correct, that they were the 'originators of Children's Movable Books', then the first book to contain pictures in which the characters could be 'made to move and act in accordance with the incidents described in each story' was one produced in 1857; and almost certainly the volume was *The Moveable Mother Hubbard*. This was subsequently advertised as No. 1 in a series of thirteen movable books; and it is to be noticed that our copy, apparently printed in 1857, carries no notices of other titles, and has the figures jointed with thread. By the beginning of 1859 Dean's had realized that the figures worked more smoothly if jointed with thin copper wire.

During the 1860s Dean's establishment at 65 Ludgate Hill must have been the scene of almost frenzied activity, of picture-colouring, of paper-sticking, of card-cutting, and of head-scratching, as they sought to keep ahead of their rivals in the field: Ward & Lock, and Darton, and Read. In 1860 they produced the first of their books of 'dissolving views' in which one picture turns into another simply by pulling a tab. By 1862 they had manu-factured movable books celebrating the feats both of Blondin and of Leotard, then the talk of London. They produced a peep-show book to display the 'lifelike effects of real distance and space'. And, at the beginning of 1863 if not earlier (though we have not found an advertisement earlier), they published the first of their 'New Scenic Books' in which, by pulling a ribbon, life was put into the cut-out figure of Little Red Riding Hood to the extent, at least, that she stood at right angles to the page. If the day of the automatic 'pop-up' book had not yet come, it wasn't far away.

A manuscript turn-up book given to a child in 1741. By lifting the first two flaps, Adam changes into a mermaid.

All the items illustrated in the next fifteen pages are in the Westerfield House Collection of Child Life and Literature.

THE ELOPEMENT
A New Harlequin Entertainment
London *Publish'd as the Act directs, April y.e 12 1771*
By Rob.t Sayer Map & Printseller N.o 53 in Fleet Street.
6.d Plain 1.s Colour'd.
Book 8.

Here Columbine in durance pent
Confiders what will Bring Content
Her Love alas! is Forc'd away
He muft not come, yet fhe muft ftay
What can She do in fuch a Plight
Turn up the Mufe will put you Right.

That Love has Wings to all is known
Which Harlequin has made his own
And at the Window like a Sprite
He Comes to View his chief Delight
Condoles her Grief which makes her moan
But you'll fee further Turn it down.

Here Columbine in durance pent
Confiders what will Bring Content
Her Love alas! is Forc'd away
He muft not come, yet fhe muft ftay
What can She do in fuch a Plight
Turn up the Mufe will put you Right.

Between 1766 and 1772 Robert Sayer produced fifteen turn-up books, most of them with theatrical or 'Harlequinade' associations. But the first, entitled *Adam and Eve*, was probably inspired by a home-made book such as that on page 65. The one here, *The Elopement*, was number 8 in the series, published April 12, 1771; and like all the others was priced '6d. Plain, 1s. Colour'd'. The title-page is shown first with both flaps down, then with the top flap lifted.

That Love has Wings to all is known
Which Harlequin has made his own
And at the Window like a Sprite
He Comes to View his chief Delight
Condoles her Grief which makes her moan
But you'll see further Turn it down.

The Antiquated Maid you see
Almost upon her bended knee
Who Cupids Arrows has defied
And all the Sports of Love beside
Peeps at the Door quite up the Stairs
And hears alike their Hopes & fears.

A Ladder made of Ropes is seen
By Harlequin to gain his Queen
The Tackle's to the Window Tyd
Down Which the Fair with Ease may Glide
Turn up & then the Rest you'll see
How these Fond Lovers both Agree.

After the top flap has been raised, the turning down of the lower flap reveals an 'Anti-quated Maid'. The story then transfers to the next two flaps, as shown, which when lifted reveal Columbine climbing down the ladder. Thereafter the lovers have trouble with Columbine's father. They evade him by suddenly appearing up a tree (to this day the plots in novelty books are incredibly weak), and the lifting of the last flap finds them unaccountably at a fair.

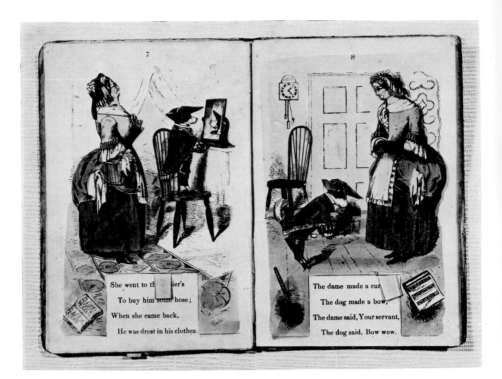

The Moveable Mother Hubbard, 1857, was the first, but not the least ambitious, of Dean's mechanical books. In the left-hand picture there are four movements, including the dog's reflection in the mirror. (Below) Dean's *Children's Sports & Pastimes*, 1861.

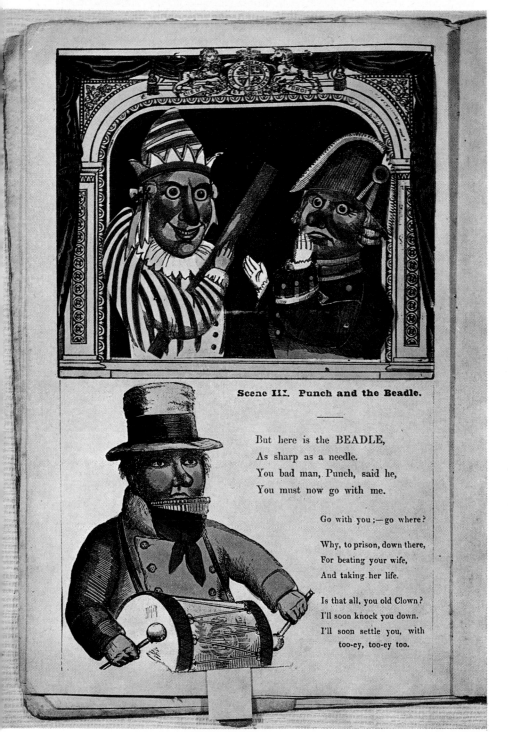

Scene III. Punch and the Beadle.

But here is the BEADLE,
As sharp as a needle.
You bad man, Punch, said he,
You must now go with me.

Go with you ;—go where?

Why, to prison, down there,
For beating your wife,
And taking her life.

Is that all, you old Clown?
I'll soon knock you down.
I'll soon settle you, with
too-ey, too-ey too.

Dean's New Moveable Book of the Boy's Own Royal Acting Punch and Judy, 1859, was the largest (14 × 9½ inches) and most satisfactory of the early animated books. It contains all the characters for a Punch and Judy show.

WAR.   PEACE.

Strife is sad, whate'er 'tis for,—
Oh, why should men delight in WAR!
Comforts, science, arts increase,
In countries where men live in PEACE.

Dean's New Book of Dissolving Views, 1860. This was the first of the 'dissolving' picture books in which, when the lower tab is pulled downwards, four slats slide behind the slats of the replacing picture.

Strife is sad, whate'er 'tis for,—
    Oh, why should men delight in WAR!
Comforts, science, arts increase,
    In countries where men live in PEACE.

The cover of *Fireside Pictures*, c. 1900, showing a child operating one of the mechanical pictures within; and *Little Red Riding Hood*, 1863, the first of 'Dean's New Scenic Books'.

(Below) One of 'Dean's Home Pantomime Toy Books,' 1880.

Ernest Nister and Raphael Tuck were the two leading publishers of novelty books at the end of the century. *Above*: Nister's *Our Peepshow*, 1897, which was printed in Bavaria.

Below: Tuck's *Country Life*, 1896, printed in Saxony. The scene has a depth of nine inches and is depicted on six planes.

The most ambitious and fragile of nineteenth-century pop-up books were the four volumes of 'Dean's Surprise Model Series' published in 1891. The effect of solidity was attempted by the use of laterally-attached cotton threads which pulled in the sides of the chief feature to make it rounded.

The brilliance of Lothar Meggendorfer's mechanical pictures lies in the coordination of the movement. In *Travels of Little Lord Thumb and His Man Damian*, 1891, Damian only just manages, each time, to escape the crocodile's jaws.

Dollies at school must not fidget at all,
Or else, like Joanna, they'll have a great fall!

Peter's an artist; oh he can paint well;
And a schoolmistress very severe is Miss Nell.

Aptly titled *Pleasant Surprises*, the change of pictures is effected by pulling ribbons which turn two discs. Published by Ernest Nister in London and by Dutton in New York, the volume was printed in Bavaria in 1914.

Dollies at school must not fidget at all,
Or else, like Joanna, they'll have a great fall!

Peter's an artist; oh he can paint well;
And a schoolmistress very severe is Miss Nell.

Three editions of *The Motograph Moving Picture Book*, in which splendidly shimmering effects are obtained by passing a piece of fine-lined talc over the pictures. The cover-picture on right is by Toulouse-Lautrec.

The *Speaking Picture Book*, with its 'characteristical voices', was looked upon as a wonder even when it was first described in 1881. 'On pulling a small button attached to the book, the noise or sound peculiar to the animal on the opened page will be emitted from under the opposite leaf.'

These nursery books of the 1920s, each about 12 inches high, are almost as much toys as books. They squeak, or have flickering eyes, or have heads which become active when the books are 'walked' along the ground. 'See me walk, See me run, Take me home, Have some fun.'

Above: Clara Vesey
Below: Miss Burnett

Above: Emily Vining
Below: Sylvia Hodson

Pin-ups of the Past

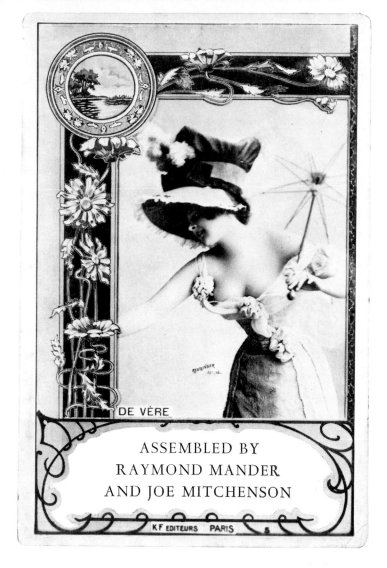

ASSEMBLED BY
RAYMOND MANDER
AND JOE MITCHENSON

DE VÈRE

K F EDITEURS PARIS

PIN-UPS, as they are now universally known, can be said to date back to the advent of commercial photography, although this title probably did not come into vogue until the First World War. Society beauties, ladies of the town, actresses from both the legitimate and the musical stage, were photographed and their pictures displayed for sale in the shops and even dispensed by slot machines for a modest price. Firstly they were a small *carte-de-visite*, later the larger cabinet-size pictures took over until the introduction of the picture post card at the turn of the century.

The four early photographs opposite are of ladies who appeared in Burlesque; not the American strip-tease 'Bur-le-que' but that strange Victorian entertainment which satirized popular plays, operas and the classics, and 'sent up' the foibles of the day.

The ladies of Burlesque and *Opéra Bouffe* were always a target for the puritan reformers. Their reputation is tacitly acknowledged in a drawing by Alfred Bryan, published in 1889, which depicts the unmistakable back of Edward, Prince of Wales, examining a playbill displayed in a pastrycook's window advertising the 'Best burlesque in London' while the shop itself is designated as a 'Noted shop for tarts'.

As Burlesque and *Opéra Bouffe* followed the transvestite tradition, the ladies played the male parts and *vice versa*; their pictures were certainly not fit for the Victorian drawing-room! Across the Atlantic Lydia Thompson, in 1868, introduced to Broadway her 'British Blondes'. Lulu Mortimer, who appeared with the rival Millie Alexandrina's 'Troupe of Blonde Beauties', is here seen in a Burlesque of the Orpheus legend being seduced by Zeus in the form of a bee.

'How would you like to swing with me?' An eighties Gaiety Girl, her shiny satin costume and boots remarkably foreshadow the kinky outfits of a later era. The first Gaiety Theatre where 'The sacred lamp of Burlesque' was lit by John Hollingshead in 1868, and was later sustained by George Edwardes, until he 'invented' musical comedy in the nineties, became legendary as the home of the 'Gaiety Girl'. These ladies of the chorus, show girls in modern parlance, have remained to this day the epitome of the naughty nineties. Darlings of the stage door Johnnies, they never stepped over the boundary of good taste into the world of the *demi-mondaine* but they and their theatre were still taboo to middle-class morality.

84

'Praise', 'Gentleness' and 'Reflection' – Edwardian book-mark post cards. These three innocent little maids could certainly be introduced into the drawing-room without bringing 'a blush of shame to the cheek of modesty', maintaining the respectability insisted upon by W. S. Gilbert (to say nothing of Sullivan) which they had introduced into the world of light opera.

The invention of the cheap picture post card, late in the nineties, opened the doors to a flood of 'pin-ups' from all over the Continent, both of celebrities and unknown models. The use of a classical pose or costume goes far back into portraiture and has always provided a convenient excuse for any innuendo!

The Greeks certainly had a word for it, but France captured the world market! Robinne as Diana, a beautiful photograph by Reutlinger, a highly reputable Parisian photographer in his day, turned into a post card for universal distribution as a *Carte postale, Cartolina postale, Tarjeta postal, Levelezolap, Postkarte* and *Briefkaart*.

The phallic innuendo of the quiver could not be mistaken even by the most innocent of recipients!

AZERAC
PARIS

DE PÉBREL

A 'Parade of the Nations' has been a standby excuse for a 'Leg show' since it was probably devised by Augustus Harris (aided and abetted by his designer, Wilhelm) when he rehabilitated Pantomime at Drury Lane in the latter years of the last century. The lady above, probably at the Folies Bergère in Paris in around 1905, represents Germany, complete with Kaiser Wilhelm on a gold Deutsches mark.

Oscar Wilde, who literally 'invented' Salome in 1892, had a lot to answer for. In the early nineteen-hundreds every dancer (the play having been banned) decided that the head of John the Baptist on a charger was a passport to success and the *Dance of the Seven Veils* proved irresistible. Maud Allen, from America, was a sensation at the Palace in London and was banned by the Watch Committee of a provincial town. Her innocence was defended by the Prime Minister of the day, Mr Asquith, who invited her to tea at No. 10! The lady on the left, Lena Barkis, looks, as Dickens would have said, 'willing'! It only needed Strauss to make Salome operatically respectable in 1905.

We now enter the realm of the 'Pose'. This rather wooden Berlin lady of 1904 (above) appears to be riding side saddle on the stump of a studio tree. A curious occupation at any time but undoubtedly provocative!

Further south, in Italy, in a warmer climate, the photographer has draped his model in tulle and given her a tiger skin on which to recline. She has given the world her 'tits' for posterity!

88

On the opposite page the same Italian photographer has posed another model on a Polar bear skin, of the kind usually reserved, anyway in this country, for infants!

The *Pose Plastique* or *Tableau Vivant* is an age-old stratagem to exploit the nude. It was used from the days of Emma Hamilton to those of The Windmill. Provided no one moved all was well. In mid-Victorian days Madame Warton titillated the town at Saville House (the site of the Empire in Leicester Square) and later Charles Morton at the Palace Theatre of Varieties found himself in trouble with the authorities over his *Tableaux Vivants*. Famous paintings were the usual excuse. *The Repentant Magdalene* by the seventeenth-century Orazio Gentileschi, at one time court painter to Charles I, must be held responsible for the 'pin-up' at the foot of the opposite page.

Of the lady on the left, above, all that can be said is that one hopes the photographer was quick off the mark and did not keep her too long in such an awkward position! Lastly, another French lady appears to have been dressed by a designer who has been reading Shakespeare's *A Midsummer Night's Dream* and taken for his inspiration 'Oh wall, O sweet and lovely wall, Show me thy chink' etc.! In this provoking position one hopes the bird behaved better than that on Nellie's hat!

Departing from the camera and entering into the realms of art these delicately tinted Viennese post cards prove much more provocative than the generally banal bathing-costumed beauties of other countries.

The seashore has naturally provided an irresistible locale for the nude in many occupations from *September Morn* onwards. After a dip in the briny a little shell music could prove acceptable; certainly modern film directors would undoubtedly find sexual connotations.

The lower lady, of the twenties, has been laid in a similar position to that of her earlier counterpart opposite, but in less public surroundings.

Once again the photographer has derived his
inspiration from a famous painting, this time
Jean-Auguste-Dominique Ingres' *La Grande Oda-
lisque*, painted in 1819. The erotic has again entered
into the realms of the artistic.

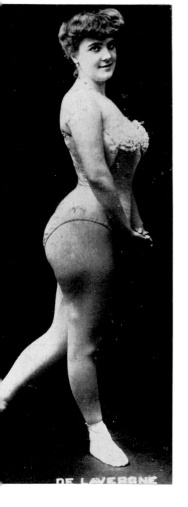

The circus, with its female acrobats and trapeze artistes, is not generally associated with 'pin-ups'; and indeed most Victorian 'female' acrobats were boys, if the truth were known; but the well-developed figure of the lady on the left warrants a place in the gallery, as does the English modern miss of the twenties in her pearls and provocative lace.

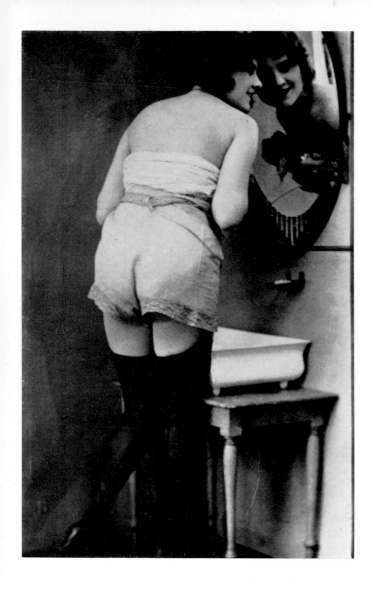

Here the French 'pin-up' begins, in the twenties, to
enter the world of the 'filthy picture' furtively
shown on the quayside to the day-tripper to Boulogne, purchased and proudly passed round among
workmates, but woe betide if the wife found a
'naughty' post card in her husband's wallet!

The cigarette for a long time was considered the hallmark of a fast woman, and daring if smoked in public, although the Victorian lady often relished a cigar in private. Even today the cigarette and sex are associated in advertisements. One wonders how such a large lady in cami-knicks managed to get herself into such a strange position 'draped' on a small set of drawers and still enjoy her cigarette!

The 'pin-up' achieves the acme of vulgarity and bad taste disguised as 'Art photography', although some would say worse was to follow in the 'Girlie' magazines of today. Is the lady at the window waiting for a tardy customer, or perhaps her lady friend is about to tickle her up with a bunch of dried twigs? The mind boggles!

The Story of Nice Nancy

Told, and illustrated from scraps, by Ronnie Barker . . . .

Nancy was a girl with a heart of gold, who went out of her way to please people. She was always smiling.

Even when she had a headache and a sore throat.

97

This sunny disposition was possibly derived from her famous ancestor, Sir Beaufort Gray, who was known to laugh a lot, even in battle.

Other attributes which endeared her to all men were her skill on the dance floor;

Her love of animals;

And the fact that she never closed her bedroom curtains.

She played on a great many musical
instruments.

She had successfully
mastered the bagpipes;

Performed beautifully on the spinet;

And had recently
taken up the organ

Her childhood had been uneventful;

She suffered the usual
childish illnesses,

Experienced the usual
            childish fears,

Kept the usual pets,

And ate the usual kinds 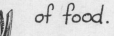 of food.

She followed the usual childhood
pursuits;

In fact, she was just an ordinary
sort of girl.

Her brother was the same.

She was a
wonderful cook,

made superb

coffee,

and her pastry was the talk of the
village.

Quite naturally, many young men visited

Nancy's house

to see what she'd
got in her oven.

Her plum puddings were
always available,

And visitors never
went away unsatisfied.

Then she met

Algernon,

a plain-clothes policeman.

Algernon was a master of disguise;

but could always be recognized by
his voice, which had a high, tinny quality.

He lived some forty miles distant,
but this did not discourage him
from visiting Nancy — he would
simply commandeer whatever form
of transport was near at hand,

and arrive at the most peculiar times.

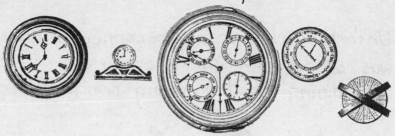

Algernon eventually decided to propose marriage to our heroine, and set out one evening to visit her, hoping to catch her before dinner.

It was early summer and as he sped along, the air was was soft and warm, and nothing was heard but the drowsy hum of insects.

He arrived at the house.

Unfortunately for all concerned, Nancy was, on that particular evening, entertaining another young man to dinner.

This young fellow had also fallen for her, after she had sent him some rather daring letters.

Nancy acted quickly, and before the echo of the door bell had died away,

her admirer was already concealed beneath a suitable piece of furniture.

Upon entering, Algernon took one look at Nancy  and immediately suspected something.

He began to inspect the room in a professional manner, through his telescope

searching for some small clue. Eventually he spotted one.

"A boot!" he deduced quickly; and a further search revealed its owner. Algernon ordered the unfortunate man to leave, in no uncertain terms.

And when the fellow refused to go,
Algernon picked him up and threw him
out of the house, clad only in his
underclothing.

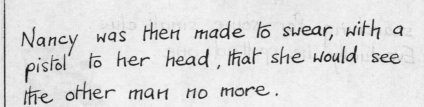

Nancy was then made to swear, with a
pistol to her head, that she would see
the other man no more.

She was, of course, full of contrition,
and tried to pacify Algernon by
offering him something to eat.

He eventually agreed to partake of
a boiled egg,

and soon appeared
to be in much
livelier spirits;

He even insisted on
washing up.

"Perhaps" said Nancy gaily, a little
later, "we might play a game this
evening, Algy."

"What did you have in mind, my
dear?" replied Algy, his eyes
lighting up in anticipation.

"An indoor game, or an outdoor game?"
"Oh, indoors, I think," she replied, giving
him a dark look.

"Have you any suggestions?"
"I can't think of anything" lied Algy,
feebly.

And so they played draughts.

Poor Algy's face was a picture of despair;

and he never forgave himself for being too shy to speak out.
Nancy was disappointed, too,
and began to despise Algernon for his lack of courage. Eventually they parted and 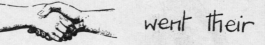 went their

separate ways;

She returned to her music,

and he became a recluse;
and regret lived with both of
them, for the rest of their lives.

That is the end of this little
tale - but I think there is a moral
to be drawn from it:-

If you desire something,
        don't hesitate!
    Jump in, feet first,
            and face the
                music!

And you will live happily, ever after it.

HOW TO BEHAVE

Drawing by Charles Keene for *Punch*, July 16, 1887

The Perfect Gentleman

BY JILLY COOPER

ETIQUETTE in other countries always seems fairly absurd. One thinks of the Japanese removing his shoes before entering the drawing-room, or the Eskimo offering the run of his unwashed wife to distinguished guests. No less foreign to our casual Western society today seems a slim volume written a hundred years ago entitled *The Complete Etiquette for Gentlemen*. Oh, the traumas of bettering oneself in those days! How one's heart bleeds for the poor tyro setting out like Christian on a tightrope journey towards social acceptability. How many Mr Salteenas must have bought the book hoping to transform themselves into the perfect gentleman – described thus:

Quietness in all things is an essential element of a well-bred person. He shuns all outward display of his personality, he cares not to be seen or heard, and rests content with being felt as a power in the land. He thus not only eschews all noisy and grandiloquent talk, but all showy and noticeable costume. His voice is low, his words simple, his action grave, and his dress plain. He holds himself so habitually under constraint that his nerves never seem to vibrate with emotion. He becomes, as it were, an impassible being [could the author have meant 'impossible'?] upon whom no external cause seems capable of making an impression.

Your perfect gentleman, in fact, is a perfect pain in the neck, one of those stodgy deadpan puddings who gazes rigid and unsmiling out of Victorian photographs. Imagine too how neurotic your tyro would become if, as well as trying to be grave, controlled, impassible, and truly well-bred, he has to follow the instructions for walking:

With your chest thrown out, your head erect, your abdomen receding rather than protruding, a self-poised and firm but elastic step, and altogether a compact, manly, homogeneous sort of bearing and movement.

Compact, manly, homogeneous, grave, his abdomen firmly receding, our tyro embarks on his first ordeal: outdoor etiquette, where he has to be permanently on his toes like St George, to protect damsels in distress.

Towards ladies the most punctilious observance of politeness is due from gentlemen. Walking with them one should, of course, assume the relative position best adapted to protect them from inconvenience or danger, and carefully note and relieve them from the approach of either.

In the next paragraph, as happens continually in the book, the heartless author dodges the issue:

No general rule can be laid down respecting offering the arm to ladies in the street . . . local custom will surely be the best guide.

Just like those infuriating cookery books which tell you to bake your cake until 'it is done'.

The truly well-bred gentleman must also remain constantly on the look-out:

Should ladies whom you know be observed unattended by a gentleman, alighting from or entering a cab or carriage, especially if there is no footman, and the driver maintains his seat, at once advance, hold the door open, and offer your hand, or protect a dress from the wheel, and bowing, pass on, all needed service rendered.

Not a word is exchanged, rather like the silent films.

An absolute ballet is involved when you meet a lady and a gentleman together:

Politeness requires that the hat should be raised as they approach, and bowing first to the ladies, include the gentleman in a sweeping motion or a succeeding bow, as the case permits. Should you stop, speak first to the lady, but do not offer to shake hands with her in full morning costume, should your glove be dark coloured or your hand uncovered. And as you part, again take your hat quite off, letting the party pass you, and on the wall side of the street, if that be practicable.

If one doesn't wish to stop as a male friend approaches, a more hearty response is recommended:

Recognise him as you advance with a smile, or 'Hope you are well, sir,' or more familiarly, 'Ah Fred [daft if he were called Nigel]. Good morning to you.'

Approaching ladies is a trickier problem; the well-bred gentleman sidles up like Grandmother's footsteps:

Be careful in hurrying forward not to incommode her, and do not speak so hurriedly or loudly as to startle her or arrest attention, and should you only have a slight acquaintance with her, say as you assume a position at her side [with elastic step and abdomen receding], 'With your permission, Madam, I will attend you', or 'Give me leave to join your walk, Miss . . .'

Of course, no well-bred man ever risks the possibility of intrusion in this way, or ever speaks first to a lady to whom he has only a passing introduction. In the latter case, you look at a lady as you advance towards her and 'await recognition'.

But don't stop walking for an instant, for only a page later the author descends like a ton of bricks on anyone who looks at ladies while standing still:

If occasion demands your remaining stationary or in the portico of a public edifice, make room at once for ladies who may be entering, and avoid any appearance of curiosity regarding them . . . make no comment even of a complimentary nature in a voice that can possibly reach their ears . . . and when walking in the street, if beauty or grace attract your attention, let your regard be respectful, and even then not too fixed.

Truly polite men are also expected to have the same reverential attitude to the arts:

In a picture gallery, at an exhibition of marbles etc. nothing can be more indicative of a want of refinement sufficient to appreciate true art, than the impertinence exhibited in audible comments upon the subjects before you; and in interfering with the enjoyment of others by passing before them, moving seats noisily, talking and laughing aloud etc. With persons of taste and refinement, there is a sacredness in the presence of genius, to desecrate which is as vulgar as it is irreverential of the beautiful and the good.

Having more or less mastered outdoor etiquette, probably at the cost of a thumping nervous break-down, our Mr Salteena now embarks on a spot of socializing. 'Among the minor obligations of social life,' says the author sternly, 'perhaps few things are regarded as more formidable by the uninitiated than ceremonious visits to ladies.' The procedure sounds rather like 'Come Dancing':

When you are shown into the Drawing Room of a private residence, if the mistress of the house is present, at once advance towards her. Should she offer her hand, be prompt to receive it, and for this purpose take your hat, stick and right hand glove in your left hand as you enter. On no account place your hat on the chairs or table.

But alas the poor reader, at this most crucial point the author rats on him again: 'There is a graceful way of holding the hat, which every well-bred man understands but which is incapable of definition.' And 'Never remain seated in the company of ladies with whom you are *ceremoniously associated*.' The language throughout the book is that of a toast master presiding over a Rotary Club Function, exhorting gentlemen in charge of ladies whose corsages groan with maidenhair fern to be 'upstanding for their President'. 'Never remain seated', but plunge into a frenzy of activity. 'Follow them to any object of interest to which they may direct your attention' (one hopes it might be a bed). 'Place a seat for them . . . ring a bell, bring a book. In short, courteously relieve them from whatever might be supposed to involve effort, fatigue or discomfort of any kind.'

Women had it so cushy in those days, one is amazed they ever wanted to be liberated. But as one never hears anything about Ladies' Liberation, perhaps it was only mere 'women' who desired a better deal.

We move now on to the dress of a gentleman for occasions of ceremony, which include a

stylish well-fitting cloth coat of some dark colour and of unexceptional quality, nether garments to correspond . . . the finest purest linen, a cravat or neckerchief, and vest of some dark or neutral tint, according to the physiognomical peculiarities of the wearer and the prevailing mode.

'Evening dress', we are told firmly, 'is never worn on Sundays, because, of course, there are no dinner parties on that day, the usual costume in all circles is a black frock coat, coloured trousers and black scarf or neck-tie.' Coloured trousers seem a bit wild for the Sabbath, particularly when the truly polite gentleman is told *never* to wear a coloured shirt because 'figures and stripes do not conceal impurity'.

An English gentleman [is also] never seen in the morning (which means all that portion of the twenty-four hours devoted to business, out-of-door amusements, and pursuits, etc.; it is always morning until the late dinner hour has passed) in the half-worn coat of fine black cloth that so inevitably gives a man a sort of shabby genteel look; but in some strong-looking rough, knock-about clothes, frequently of nondescript form and fashion.

He also had to tread a fine line between hippy and skinhead:

If you wear your beard, wear it in moderation – extremes are always vulgar. Avoid all fantastic arrangements of the hair, either turning it under in a roll, or allowing it to straggle over the coat collar, or having it cropped so close as to give the wearer the appearance of a sporting character.

(What vapours the author would have had over today's long-haired sporting characters kissing each other after goals are scored!)

Dining out must have struck terror in the most confident student of society – rather like taking one's finals.

Nothing more plainly shows the well-bred man than his manners at table. A man may be well dressed, may converse well but if he is after all unrefined, his manners at table will expose him. If he is *au fait* at dinner he has passed one of the severest tests of good breeding.

All the things one had to remember *not* to do: one mustn't evidently eat ice cream with a spoon (what happened if it melted?) or asparagus with one's fingers, or drink one's soup noisily, or put butter on one's vegetables, or gape at others, or twist about, or 'give too insanguined pieces of meat to ladies' (rather like the Americans offering the 'white meat' instead of the breast).

It was also evidently a breach of etiquette to repeat the name of any person with whom one was conversing. Think of the clangers Tennyson dropped in 'Come into the garden, Maud'. Conversation must have been a nightmare too: 'One is sure', says the author smugly, 'to show good or bad breeding the instant one opens one's mouth.' Well-bred people, it seemed, never discussed politics or anything remotely highbrow ('with ladies, agreeability rather than profundity should be your aim') or last night's party, or any of one's friends ('gentlemen never assail absent ones in mixed parties'). One couldn't, obviously, talk about sex:

Anything that will crimson the cheek of true womanhood is unworthy and unmanly to a degree of which it is not easy to express sufficient abhorrence.

All a bit Wet-iquette.

'Good jokes and merriment', however, were 'always in order'. God knows what they found to make them about.

But all strained attempts at facetiousness by one who has not a natural talent for it, are sure to end in making him ridiculous. Therefore, let no man venture upon gay sallies at dinner, unless they so press forward to his lips as to escape almost in spite of him.

It is not surprising gay sallies pressed forward at dinner bearing in mind the amount of drink everyone knocked back. 'Always hurry the bottle round five or six times . . . and if either lady or gentleman is invited to take wine at table, he or she must never refuse.' The ritual of taking wine is straight out of Rotarian Ladies' Night:

You should politely say: 'Shall I have the pleasure of a glass of wine with you?' You will then either hand him the bottle, or send it by the waiter and afterwards fill your own glass, when you politely and silently bow to each other as you raise the wine to your lips.

All very gracious and decorous and manly, which makes it all the more of a shock when, in the next chapter, the author suddenly plunges into a panegyric rivalling the most unbridled flights of women's romantic fiction:

Are there any good reasons why the subject of love should be shrouded in mystery, for it is the one which occupies more than all others the human thoughts. We think not.

Poetry is filled with it. Romance is replete with it, the drama – tragic, comic or operatic, turns on it. It is the most interesting theme of society.

A brisk broadside is then fired at male chauvinism:

Clubs where men meet to read newspapers, talk politics, dine and play together are *not* society [and] tea parties and other exclusive assemblances of the ladies are *not* society. These are its severed halves which require to come together, and the charm which draws them together, in its purest form, and its highest expression, is the passion of love.

At last our tyro may get a chance to embark on gay sallies, in his fashionable vest of some dark or neutral tint.

A young man entering society at the age when young men begin to be desirable members – which is not until they are capable of the tender passion – is likely to be attracted by one or more persons. [Sounds a bit promiscuous.]

The first attraction of a very young man is likely to be to a lady of mature years, and this sentiment when it can be indulged without ridicule or scandal, and has for its object a woman of taste and character is great good fortune. Such a woman is just the teacher and friend a young man needs to polish his manners, refine his taste, improve his understanding and ripen his heart.

At this point one suddenly begins to suspect that the author is no gentleman at all, but a rather sour, middle-aged lady of mature years, whose husband spends too much time at his club, and who rather fancies the idea of young men languishing after her. One sees her as a sort of Tabitha Twitchet, permanently worrying how the fine company will react, and terrified that wild, boisterous kittenish people are going to rush in and spoil the dignity and repose of her tea party.

Her rash fierce blaze of riot doesn't last, anyway. Poetry and drama may be filled with the passion of love, but our well-bred truly polite tyro isn't going to be so lucky. 'A love affaire ought to be conducted with caution and delicacy, there should be no rashness or mistake', we are told, and when you have been accepted and the engagement announced, 'Be discreet in your raptures, and begin preparing with all diligence and dignity for the change that awaits you.' (Rather like going into the church.)

Nor is anyone going to get the chance to marry a smasher. 'A career of idleness and irresponsibility' (with men charging about fetching books, ringing bells, carrying shawls for her, one doesn't see how she could have had anything else) 'is no desirable prelude to the quiet duties essential to the home happiness of a man of moderate resources and retired habits. It may be questioned whether a woman who has long been used to the adulation and excitement of a crowd will be content . . . with the simple pleasures which alone will be at her command thus circumstanced.'

The gates of the prison house begin to close:

However gay and frivolous a man may have been before his engagement, he should conduct himself with the utmost propriety after that event. A sense of what is due to a lady should repress all habits disagreeable to her, smoking if she dislikes it, frequenting places of amusement without her, paying attention to other women. Nothing is so disgusting as the flirtations which some men carry on after they have pledged themselves to one alone.

Shades of *The Desert Song*! Then the old double standard emerges again. 'Women may have some excuse for coquetry, but a man has none.' The husband, however, gets his own back on the day of the wedding:

The etiquette of the wedding breakfast varies considerably in good circles. The bride may appear at the breakfast or not, but the latter procedure is generally preferred.

Presumably while the husband is getting sloshed with all his friends and relations the bride is expected to sit alone in her bedroom contemplating the horrors of the impending night.

Once they are married, one of the 'quiet duties' of the bride will surely be shopping, and there is stern advice on the subject. 'It is seldom indeed that a lady of any refinement delays long in making her purchases.' In her husband too, one of the most heinous crimes is chatting up shop girls:

It is remarkable how little some men can be, how childish, although adorned with hirsute appendages and looking, as far as the outer man goes, intelligent. Yet their talk is all lisped nothings. Their eyes sparkle as they lisp the silliest things; they laugh and make merry, and cause people to turn in wonder that any human being could make himself so thoroughly ridiculous; and they 'chaff the girls' to use their own vulgar phraseology, until it has occurred to them that a change of scene would be productive of new delights.

Your well-bred man is also a lightning shopper, like his wife:

A man of sense and good taste loses no more time than is necessary in making a purchase, and what he says is to the purpose.

If, on the other hand, any shop girl starts chatting *him* up, she is firmly slapped down:

Should he perceive a disposition on the part of the assistant to entertain him with a little small talk, he very politely disregards it by an allusion to the article bought, and leaves. He can be on no terms of familiarity with one whose only title to address him at all is his presence as a buyer, but this is shown in such a way that he leaves the impression that his conduct is that of a well-bred man.

On to the ballroom, where fatties and clodhoppers go to the wall:

It is far preferable to be a passive spectator than a clumsy performer. It may be said, also, that while a knowledge of dancing adds to the attraction of a figure naturally symmetrical and agile, it serves but to render still more conspicuous those who are incurably ill-shaped, heavy, or insensible to any graceful motion.

Even if you do dance well, you've got to watch it:

Move quietly, do not kick or caper about, nor sway your body to and fro; perform your steps easily, and lead the lady as lightly as you would tread a measure with a spirit of gossamer.

The spirit of gossamer has also got to watch out that she only waltzes with 'one worthy of so close an intimacy'.

For a gentleman waltzing with a lady, there is skittish advice. He should beware not to press her waist: 'You must only lightly touch it with the palm of your hand, lest you leave a disagreeable impression, not only on her ceinture, but on her mind.' Waltzing is also 'proper and agreeable as the pleasant exercise of a morning, where in a family group' (the men presumably in strong-looking knock-about clothes of nondescript form and fashion) 'the piano forte is opened and the dance occupies the pauses of conversation' (a hell of a lot of them, one would think, when there is so little subject matter) 'and gives life and motion to those who so often grow languid and ill for want of it.'

A gentleman of feeling [we are told] will not fail to lead out a lady who appears to be neglected by others, but he will not do it ostentatiously.

One is reminded of Mr Knightly saving Harriet from humiliation, when Mr Elton refused to dance with her. Mr Knightly is probably the only really attractive man in nineteenth-century fiction that the author would have approved of. Mr Rochester and Heathcliff wouldn't have stood a chance, nor Will Ladislaw skulking in the laurels, and certainly not Sidney Carton, nor Mr Darcy, spurning Elizabeth Bennett at the Assembly rooms.

A gentleman, too, should take it like a man if a lady turns him down.

We cannot always fathom the hidden springs which influence a woman's actions, and there are many bursting hearts within white satin dresses; therefore do not insist upon the fulfilment of established rules.

There is also advice about public balls:

If you are entirely a stranger, it is to the stewards or Master of Ceremonies you must apply for a partner, quickly of course [like shopping], any young lady with whom you should like to dance when, if there is no obvious inequality of rank, you will be presented for that purpose; should there be an objection, someone who is considered more suitable [probably the boss-eyed daughter of the Master of Ceremonies] will be selected for you.

But watch your step next day:

Any presentation to a lady in a public ballroom for the mere purpose of dancing does not entitle you to claim her acquaintance afterwards; therefore should you meet her, at most you may lift your hat; but even that is better avoided, unless, indeed, she first bows – as neither she nor her friends can know who or what you are.

You may easily have turned into a bumpkin at midnight.

We then move on to mannish pursuits, the gentleman in his club, where we find Old Stuffed Shirt: 'The well-bred man of the world who has seen everything and done everything, who is surprised at nothing, and believes only in stern facts.' One rubs shoulders with some reprehensible types: 'The rather boisterous youngster who has just commenced to mix with men', and 'the sallow skinned Anglo-Indian who is reserved by reason of his liver' (perhaps it was the *Plat de jour*).

To watch the entrance of Stuffed Shirt, we are told, is always a profitable study; as usual, he never puts an elastically stepping foot wrong. We notice his 'quiet dignity' as he walks to his accustomed seat, nodding to a friend here and another there, as he is perceived. And when he wants a drink 'this is done in the quietest possible way' (all well-bred men seem to be members of the Noise Abatement Society). 'No rapping on the table with a stick or coin; the bell is pulled without violence but just so that it can be heard. It is the height of rudeness to let everybody know you are about to partake of refreshment.'

One is also advised to temper stinginess with altruism in good Forsyte style:

If your guest prefers claret to champagne, let him have claret by all means. To say to him 'have something better' implies that he has only been accustomed to drink which is inexpensive, and that on this occasion you will give him a treat.

In the smoking room, it goes without saying, the conversation should be carried on so as not to disturb your neighbour:

As a rule middle class Englishmen rarely offend in this way . . . so much cannot be said for our continental friends, notwithstanding the name they have earned for politeness. Their presence is felt and their tongues are heard on the threshold of the place, and they talk and gesticulate the whole evening, as though their affairs were the only ones of importance in the world. It is well for us that we do not imitate them, otherwise there would be neither decorum nor comfort to be found anywhere outside one's bedroom.

Decorum in the bedroom? However did Victorian couples produce a Tertius, a Sextus or even an Octavius?

But if the Victorians would have been shocked by the sexual freedom of the twentieth century, equally shocking to us today is the way the Victorians sanctioned the making of money. The author praises 'Acquisitiveness' as a most gentlemanly virtue.

To acquire and gather wealth, to create riches by industry, to accumulate a wealth of beautiful things is a high right and duty of every person. To be honestly rich, to be rich with a full recognition of the rights of others is noble and praiseworthy in all respects.

It sounds like a credo for the Forsytes. Presumably in their spare time they trained camels to jump through the eye of a needle. *The Complete Etiquette for Gentlemen* is in fact a book in praise of bourgeois gentility. The upper classes are continually being cut down to size.

There is no more common or absurd mistake than to suppose if people are of high rank they cannot be ill-bred . . . even the lower classes (whatever their own practices may be) keenly appreciate and gratefully acknowledge the slightest consideration shown to them by their superiors.

One suspects more than a touch of resentment towards all those grand unmanageable people who couldn't give a fig about etiquette and went round doing exactly what they liked.

Drawing by Charles Keene for *Punch*, June 13, 1885

The Perfect Lady

BY ARTHUR MARSHALL

'CAN ANYTHING in the world be nicer than a really nice girl?' asked Mrs Humphry ('Madge' of *Truth*). Well, various possible answers spring to mind, but Mrs Humphry, who wrote about *Manners for Women* towards the close of the Victorian age and whose praiseworthy aim it was to keep ladies firmly on the acceptable social tracks, clearly expected by way of reply a resounding, deafening NO. The modern girl, lolloping her way down the King's Road in clothes plainly filched from her great-grandmother's wardrobe, may care to profit from Mrs Humphry's explanations as to what, at the turn of the century, constituted a really nice girl, and a girl, moreover, about to burgeon into glorious womanhood, marry and become a perfect lady. Etiquette books of the period are numerous and provide valuable signposts to a leisured life of refinement and good taste.

First, the voice. You'll probably have to change it. Nothing even faintly shrill will do. Sweet and low is the best. The thing to aim at is a mellow contralto, the muted boom of a pocket Clara Butt with the vocal chords revolving sluggishly in a sort of gearbox of liquid honey and producing a restricted range of ear-caressing tones. And with the voice, the laugh. This needs practice. Don't imagine for a single solitary moment that your laugh is all right. It isn't. But courage! Help is at hand. Genial Mrs Humphry leaps once more to the rescue and urges us to follow the example of the actress, Miss Florence St. John, who every morning 'sings a descending octave staccato with the syllables Ha! Ha! Ha!' Mrs Humphry doesn't say *where* she does this but you'll soon find a secluded spot – the small billiard-room, the second sitting-room or the orangery would all be quite suitable. Close the door, clear the throat and let fly 'with a ripple of silvery notes that form the perfect laugh'. Tight-waisted corsets, though showy enough in their way, are at this moment no sort of help. Either loosen them or ring for your maid and totally remove them and start again.

Those who cannot master the St. John laugh are in for really frightful trouble. Mrs Humphry, hard as nails when necessary, is merciless in her strictures of the deplorable 'He! He!', the double chuckle 'Ho! Ho!', and the 'Haw! Haw!' 'which instantly reveals the self-conscious air of the underbred'. Needless to say, 'Madge' doesn't even so much as mention giggles and titters, both being beneath contempt and best ignored completely.

After approximately three months of Florence St. John and ditto of Clara Butt, we are just about ready to speak and, indeed, to laugh, should a tasteful opportunity present itself. Yes, but speak about what? Here we desert Mrs Humphry, if it be but temporarily, and fly for aid to 'A Member of the Aristocracy' who, having fallen maybe on evil and impecunious days, produced an admirable volume entitled *Society Small Talk*. In no time at all it had sold 80,000 copies and unleashed, up and down the country, thunderclaps of excited, breezy chatter.

Don't, counsels Our Member of the Aristocracy, attempt too much too soon. Nothing is to be gained by haste. Girls cannot run before they can walk. Eschew, naturally, the vapid and vacant manner, and be all lively attention, with the eyes opened wide and the lips freshly moistened, but limit yourself, until you find your feet, to either 'Really?' or 'Indeed!' Then ring the changes. After a month or so of 'Really?' and 'Indeed!' you are ready for bigger things. Nothing too ambitious, you understand, but, for once, a direct statement. Choose a cosy-looking lady and, for pity's sake, keep the voice down. 'I always think it is a good plan to go to the sea in November. The sunny mornings are so invigorating and cheering, are they not?', which may well lead on to a spirited exchange of opinions concerning the rival residential merits of Eastbourne and Scarborough (on no account mention Brighton if there is any risk at all of being misunderstood). Why Our Member plumps for the month of November, or just where she finds her sunny mornings, it is not for us to question.

Before passing on to other invaluable conversational ball-rollers, Our Member gives a most helpful list of Remarks To Avoid, helpful because they are all just the kind of thing that one might have clumsily, as they say, come out with. For example, 'How painfully dissipated and extravagant your son appears to be. What a wasted career his is.' The lady thus addressed may well find herself, while reeling from this body-blow, the victim of a follow-up attack: 'What a very unbecoming colour green is to you. I wonder why you wear it.' And then, by way of laying her flat on the canvas: 'How drawn and pale your husband looks. Is he quite well?'

Back to jollier matters and the sort of chit-chat one will be likely to find in the upper-crust world in which one is, of course, most at ease. How's this for starters? 'I understand Lord Lynton's illness was entirely owing to drinking iced water. It gave a very severe shock to his entire system and he is recovering in Baden Baden.' A sympathetic mumbling sound will suffice by way of answer, and then it's your turn: 'What really gorgeous diamonds Mrs Chetwynd wore last night, but who was the woman with the black pearls?' Who indeed? But there is no time to discover her identity, for dinner has just been announced and the procession of pairs is forming up. You need something to say while parading to the dining-room? Very well then. 'We must take care not to tread upon the Duchess's smart train. We do not want to bring the wrath of the fair wearer down upon our heads! She is in great looks *ce soir*, is she not?'

Before passing on to a really magnificent sheaf of lively opening remarks, Our Member, reminding us that both yawning and glazed expressions are not in good taste, gives excellent advice on how to extricate yourself from a boring dinner-table conversation with the man on your right, thus: 'Your friend opposite appears to be relating something amusing. What is he saying?', and while the bore is politely trying to discover what the jape was, swing sharply round to the man on your left with 'Where are you quartered just now?'

But to our openers, and what a feast of ingenuity they are, ranging from shorties such as 'Have you a leaning towards spiritualism?' and 'What have you to say in favour of stimulants?' to more robust stuff: 'What wonderful strides oculists have made in late years. The aurists are very much behind in their discoveries in the sister art! How trying it can be to talk to deaf persons...', which leads comfortably on to a discussion of ear-trumpets and the new and vastly improved Luxivox 'Stentor' silver-plated model. After this, the pace quickens excitingly: 'Have you been to the Academy? I hope we are to hear you sing later. I see that the next tempting *entrée* is sweetbreads! Do you paint on china? Do you model in soap? Are you fond of balls?'

'When friendship outsteps its prescribed limits', coyly announces our informant, 'it enters upon Cupid's domain.' Dan Cupid is by no means skimped in her social survey and finds his fullest expression among the dreamy waltzes ('Do you reverse?') and the glossy palms of the ballroom. 'How well the rooms are lighted', says the girl, with perhaps a romantic wish for less dazzling illuminations, while the man, inflamed with claret-cup, counters meaningfully with 'Yes, they are lighted by the light of beauty's eyes, and you are lending your share!' The girl flaps her fan a little (she isn't going to swoon *yet*) and cries, 'Now, Captain Anstruther, that was a deliberate compliment!', to which the obvious riposte, and one hardly needs to set it down, is 'I envy that butterfly perched so daintily on your hair close to that shell-like ear. What secrets would I not whisper were I so near. Happy butterfly!'

Nothing, incidentally, is easier, on sultry nights, than to keep the ballroom deliciously cool. 'Simply remove all the windows and place large blocks of ice in every convenient spot', and please don't make difficulties where no difficulties are.

But stay! Before Cupid's darts start to find their mark, what has been going on at the dinner-table itself? The guests are assembled there, after all, mainly to eat. Let us follow the fortunes of the lady who has, we trust, succeeded in not impeding the Duchess's sedate progress foodwards. She seats herself where instructed, hastily whips off her gloves, placing them carefully on the table without disturbing the fronds of virginia creeper that have been spread tastefully here and there, unfolds her napkin, places the piece of bread it contained at her *left* hand, fires off an opener ('I understand that the Bishop has supplied our Vicar, fortunate man, with a new tricycle'), and is now all ready to tackle soup and, mind you, just the half ladleful ('To fill a soup-plate with soup would be in very bad style', warns Our Aristocrat.)

The process of munching, the manipulation of cutlery and the general eating accoutrements all bristle with traps and problems. 'However handsome a cruet-stand may be, it should never be placed on the dinner-table.' There now! and one had been going to place it bang in the middle and cover it with smilax. 'When peas are partaken of, convey them to the mouth with the *fork*' and don't attempt to balance them on the knife. At no point may the knife be placed *in* the mouth, and to prong an edible with the point of the knife would be the act of a complete outsider.

With the arrival of the meat and vegetable course, Our Member becomes very agitated and communicates her anxieties to her readers. There is so much here that can go wrong; one can hardly hold the knife for nervous trembling. '*Don't* overload the fork. Convey meat and vegetables to the mouth *separately*'; don't arrange them on the fork in a compact form. The hand and the mouth 'should act in unison. The mouth should *not* be kept open in expectation of the well-laden fork's arrival. The mouth should only be opened to receive the contents of the fork at the moment when it has reached the lips.' Safe at last, you think? Not at all. 'To place the fork directly opposite the mouth is a most ungraceful way of eating, and bending the wrist round to accomplish this feat is similarly so. The fork should be simply raised to the mouth, and the hand should *not* be turned round to face it.' All this, and conversation too! ('Which are your favourites among the grasses and ferns of Great Britain?')

Let us mark time for a moment and return to the good Mrs Humphry to garner an assorted bundle of useful hints to help one along Life's Highway. Are you recently a widow? If so, you may now wear linen collars a month after your bereavement – previously you would have had to wait six months for linen collars; so, while sorrowing, be grateful for small mercies. Is your daughter about to be married? In that case, on no account order too *heavy* a cake, 'heavy' in the sense of sheer weight ('They have been known to bring down both the table on which they rested and the ceiling of the room beneath'). If you *must* bicycle, do beware of 'the promiscuous acquaintanceship for which the handy steeds are frequently responsible': don't set out awheel

unless fully kitted up – inability to mend punctures gives a man
a chance to pounce and indulge in almost any sort of familiarity
('Can I lend you my pump?'). When yachting, fight down that
urge 'to don lace-trimmed white petticoats', and for punting,
heel-less prunella shoes just will not do: 'neat patents' are the
thing. Oh, and in the Casino at Deauville do remember that
men, and foreign men at that, with their bold, unbridled,
challenging glances, may be standing behind your chair: so
avoid too generous a *décolletage*.

And now, for all these splendidly varied activities, what are
you going to *wear*? There is no end to the exciting range of
possibilities for girls just 'out' and for ladies of riper years –
married ladies, of course (it is sad but true that nowhere in any
of the books is the smallest attention paid to spinsters. As a
class, they do not, however well-born, exist). Fancy-dress balls
are all the rage, so why not startle your circle of friends by going
as a hot-blooded Bacchante in mauve accordion-pleated chiffon,
your bodice prettily draped with grapes and vine leaves, and
pearls and beads wound into your *coiffure*. And that is not all.
Mrs Eric Pritchard, a mine of information on this and other
subjects, advises that the costume be completed 'by the skin of
a lynx arranged on the front of the dress. This gives a wild and
fantastic touch.' Yes indeed. Best to order half a dozen lynx
skins and keep them handy. You never know when they'll be
needed.

There's not the faintest need to look dowdy while motoring,
so why not a threequarter-length *Directoire* coat in puce velvet,
your beaded bag jammed with smelling-salts in case of a spill
from the De Dion Bouton, and on your head a bright green
beaver toque trimmed with black braid cockades? For rail travel
(and hold on to that bag in case of a derailment at Devizes) a
smart tailor-made is the ideal thing, 'with a beautifully cut
waistcoat of white leather with the bolero coat turned back with
revers of green and gold embroidery and with a short basque
over the hips. There is a certain studied simplicity about this
garment', muses Mrs Pritchard, 'which renders it particularly
striking' (she does not, alas, inform us about what would, in
her view, constitute a complicated garment). For country walks

'the *trotteuse* skirt is still *de rigueur*, accompanied by the neatest and smartest footgear', while for the bridge table get your *couturière* to run you up a Josephine robe in Liberty velveteen and Indian muslin.

A few years behind Mrs Humphry, but spiritually at one with her – two cherries on one stalk – proudly marches Mrs Massey Lyon, with a positive cornucopia of wide-ranging instruction for those tip-toeing cautiously about in society's upper reaches. If invited to a Royal garden party, don't for goodness' sake go and plonk yourself down in the special 'Durbar' tent and start wolfing the cress sandwiches (they are intended for the Royal teeth). If Royalty comes to dine with *you*, do remember that the sovereign and consort are the only ones allowed finger-bowls at dessert. (Why?) And if the German Emperor comes to stay, your house will have to absorb a retinue of not less than eighty people, thirty of whom will expect private sitting-rooms.

In a thought-provoking chapter entitled Little Things That Count, Mrs Massey Lyon prefers 'May I have the salt, please?' to 'May I trouble you for the salt?', and '*Au revoir*' makes a pleasant change from 'Good-bye' and shows that the week-end at Boulogne was not wasted. In country houses, where morning and evening prayers are said in the private chapel, always attend unless (rather mysteriously) asked not to. It is good form for men to take off their hats in hotel lifts if ladies are present but they should keep their hats *on* in hotel corridors. Don't say 'Pray assist yourself to whisky', and a handy sentence for almost any English occasion is 'Escaped the 'flu fiend, I trust?' Oh, and do get names pronounced correctly. 'Beauchamp' is 'Beechum', 'Lygon' is 'Liggon' and 'Pontefract', as with those delicious cakes, is 'Pomfret'.

Well now, I think that's everything. All set, Jennifer? O.K., Mrs Budibent? Off you go then, and good luck. As you see, there's really nothing to it.

PERSONAL PAGES

'One after another they came at me'

The Victorian Crusoe

BY BEVIS HILLIER

'THE KEY-NOTE of the Magazine is struck in the motto on the cover – "Truth is Stranger than Fiction",' said the editorial of the first issue of the *Wide World Magazine* in April 1898. 'This we hope to prove by personal narratives and actual photographs. Also on the cover you will read "Astounding Photographs" – "Thrilling Adventures". Big words, these. Do the Contents of this first number justify such phrases? It is for our readers to judge.'

In the two years before scandal brought it to an untimely end, the magazine published such articles as 'The Romance of Seal Hunting' by Sir George Baden-Powell, 'The Perils of [General] Gordon's Postman', 'A Battle Royal with a Tiger' by A. Sarath Kumar Ghosh, 'How I Discovered the Great Devil-Fish' by Rev. M. Harvey, LL.D., 'Picnics in Perak', 'The Fiery Ordeal of Fiji', 'Nearly Eaten', 'Savages at Play' and 'How Our Baby Was Stolen by Baboons'.

Today the magazine is best remembered (and sold at high prices by dealers in second-hand books) for an early and characteristically mendacious article by 'Baron Corvo' (Frederick Rolfe) – 'How I Was Buried Alive'. The article purported to describe how the future author of *Hadrian the Seventh*, sent into a cataleptic trance by a lizard running up his sleeve ('I have a horror of all creeping things'), had been taken for dead and nailed in a coffin by the friars in whose care he was convalescing from an illness. The first page of the article carries a photograph of a crop-haired Corvo nonchalantly smoking a cigarette.

In *The Quest for Corvo* (1943) A. J. A. Symons reprinted the attack on Corvo which appeared in the *Aberdeen Free Press* in November 1898, shortly after the *Wide World* article. It exposed Corvo as Rolfe, and listed several of his peccadilloes; the story is more fully told in Donald Weeks's 1971 biography of Corvo. But already, before the Corvo episode, the *Wide World Magazine* had been publicly ridiculed for publishing a series of articles by a far more extravagant impostor. In its exposé of Corvo the *Aberdeen Free Press* wrote:

The world was recently startled by the discovery by the *Wide World Magazine* – a new periodical devoted to the promulgation of true statements of thrilling adventure – of a greater than Robinson Crusoe in the person of M. Rougemont, and a little later the public was equally amused when it was shown what manner of man that great explorer and anthropologist really is. Being about done with the Rougemont affair, the *Wide World Magazine* has discovered another personage. . . .

Louis de Rougemont claimed to have been born in or near Paris in 1844 – to give an historical tally, the same year as Gerard Manley Hopkins and Andrew Lang. He was educated (his account continues) in Switzerland, where he and his school-fellows took a keen interest in geology. When he was about nineteen his mother gave him some 7,000 francs and he set out for Cairo, intending eventually to visit French possessions in the Far East. He stayed in Egypt only a few days and then set out for Singapore. There (1863) he met a Dutch pearl fisher named Jensen who had a small forty-ton schooner at Batavia. Jensen wanted to organize a trip to some virgin pearling grounds off the south of New Guinea, but lacked the necessary capital. De Rougemont took the hint and joined him. Having taken on stores at Batavia – Rougemont insisted on tinned food and ship's biscuits – they sailed to the islands of the Dutch archipelago and took on forty experienced Malay divers: Jensen tested them by making them dive for bright pieces of tin. The final crew numbered forty-four and a dog, Bruno. In the fishing grounds the Malays dived, and Rougemont's job was to stay on board, open the shells, and credit each diver with his catch. The divers were rewarded with food, chutney, rum, tobacco and 'Brummagem' jewellery – never with money. At one point they were attacked by boatloads of Papuan natives, whom Captain Jensen had offended by not allowing them on board after bartering. The Malays, alarmed by this incident and by the attack of a marauding octopus, petitioned the captain to leave that region, and the boat moved on to some more unexplored fishing grounds. Here three black pearls were discovered in one shell, and Jensen was so excited (the black pearls being worth almost as much as all the others put together) that he insisted on remaining at sea longer than was advisable. The pearling season was almost ended and the yearly cyclonic changes were actually due, but the captain had the 'pearl fever' and refused to budge. The aneroid 'began jumping about in a very uneasy manner' but Jensen took no notice.

'And now', wrote Rougemont, 'I pass to the fatal day that made me an outcast from civilization for so many weary years.' One morning in July 1864 Jensen went off with the whole crew, leaving only Rougemont and the dog aboard. Already that morning a tidal wave had broken over the stern, flooding the cabins; but Jensen had merely put the pumps to work and had not taken the warning. A terrific storm broke, and Rougemont helplessly watched the captain's two pearling boats drift away. 'The climax was reached about two o'clock, when a perfect cyclone was raging.' He never saw the captain or the Malays again. The ship's charts had been destroyed by flood, but he took observations from the sun and steered due west, then west by south, hoping to come upon one of the islands of the Dutch Indies, such as Timorland. But no land came into sight. Just before dark on the evening of the thirteenth day he saw an island in the distance ('Melville Island, I now know it to be'). He could see the smoke of many fires, and as he drew nearer, saw several natives, 'perfectly nude, running wildly about on the beach and brandishing their spears in my direction'. In Apsley Strait, between Melville and Bathurst Islands, he was rained on by spears and boomerangs, but escaped.

Some time between the fifteenth and twentieth days the ship was wrecked on a coral reef. Rougemont was thrown heavily to the deck and through a blow on the head became temporarily stone deaf. He loosened some casks and chests in the hope that they would wash ashore. Then he and the dog swam for the sandbanks. Exhausted by the breakers, Rougemont clutched the dog's tail and was tugged ashore. When the seas had calmed he swam out to the ship and obtained a tomahawk, bow and arrows, some water, tinned food and flour. He built a hut of pearl shells. He began building a boat and screamed with delight when it floated; only to find that he had launched the heavy craft in a kind of lagoon several miles in extent, barred by a crescent of coral rocks over which he alone could not possibly drag the boat into the open sea. He kept himself amused by acrobatics, riding turtles, sailing about the lagoon in the boat, and beating a drum made of sharkskin stretched over a barrel.

A family of 'four blacks' was driven ashore on his strip of island. Rougemont revived the half-drowned natives with rum, and made good friends with the woman and two boys, though the father, Gunda, always treated him with antagonism, as Rougemont offended him 'by declining to take advantage of a certain embarrassing offer which he made me soon after his recovery'. In the last week of May 1866 they all sailed off in the big boat (which could be lifted over the reef by all of them) in an attempt to reach the mainland. They landed once on an island – 'probably Baker Island, in the vicinity of Admiralty Gulf'. When, eventually, they reached the mainland, a great *corroboree* was held by the natives.

The next big event was Rougemont's enforced marriage to 'a young, dusky maiden of comparatively pleasing appearance'. In the ceremony he was given a large club, and imagined he was being invited to club her to death as preliminary to a cannibal feast, but later realized he was only to tap her head as symbol of her subjection. He then exchanged wives with Gunda, as he had taken a great fancy to Gunda's intelligent thirty-year-old wife, Yamba.

Rougemont gives lurid descriptions of native food, which included rats and frizzled worms, and also of a cannibal feast. ('I saw mothers with a leg or an arm surrounded by plaintive children, who were crying for their portion of the fearsome dainty.') Turning to something 'more amusing', as he put it, he described how women settled their differences by taking turns in hitting each other with a huge club 'until one of the unfortunate, stoical creatures fell bleeding and half-senseless to the earth'. One terrible adventure was harpooning a baby whale by mistake: its mother 'bore down upon us like a fair-sized island rushing through the sea with the speed of an express train', with the result that their boat was smashed to fragments.

Both the baby whale and the mother whale who stayed by its side were stranded by the tide; Rougemont got the credit for this exploit from the natives, who gorged themselves on blubber and

'I then shot-half-a-dozen arrows into the enemy's ranks.'

made themselves ill. He won additional prestige for killing a large alligator with his tomahawk and afterwards wore a circlet of alligator teeth on his head. He and Yamba now set off on the long trek towards civilization, armed with a 'passport stick' scratched with cabbalistic characters, which he also wore in his hair. They struggled through deserts of spinifex ('porcupine grass'), and suffered agonies of thirst, finally quenched when Rougemount heard a mystic voice intoning *'Coupe l'arbre!'* (it was an 'Australian bottle tree' and liquid gushed out). He now made a serious geographical error. Thinking he was near Cape York Peninsula, when in fact he was on the west coast of the Gulf of Carpentaria, he decided to strike due north, instead of south, using a dug-out canoe. He expected to reach Somerset, a white settlement he had heard about from the pearlers. In fact he arrived, after leaving the mouth of the Roper River, at Point Dale, and steered between the mainland and Elcho Island. Thinking this was the little strait between Albany Island and Cape York, he then steered south-west, but eventually found himself heading straight for the native settlement of Yamba's people which they had left weeks before. The natives cried with joy, and Rougemont decided to stay among them for a while to recuperate. His new exploits included leading Yamba's tribe against an unfriendly tribe: he frightened them away by appearing on stilts with his bow and arrow.

Setting off again, they came upon a black chief who had two frightened nude white girls in captivity as his 'wives'. Rougemont asked for a parley with him and got to the girls a message pricked on a water-lily leaf: 'A Friend is Near, Fear Not'. He wrestled with the chief for the two girls, and killed him, much to the approval of the chief's tribesmen, when the chief attempted a foul hit. 'The body of the chief was not eaten (most likely on account of the cowardice he displayed).' Rougemont made clothes for the girls, Blanche and Gladys Rogers; learnt Moore's songs, and played rounders with them to the natives' astonishment.

Now Rougemont and his entourage set off on the last lap of their journey; and here begins a killing-off of *dramatis personae* only rivalled by the end of *Hamlet*: first the two girls are drowned, then Rougemont's two half-caste children, always weaker than their native playmates, expire; then poor Yamba gets very wrinkled and suddenly perishes; finally Bruno gives his last pathetic wuff and tailwag. The reason, of course, is that Rougemont is nearing journey's end (and the offices of the *Wide World Magazine*) and has to 'write out' of the story the characters he can't produce.

There were a few more adventures before Rougemont rejoined civilization. He sighted a ship and approached it with an escort of natives on catamarans – only to be fired on by the ship, whose captain evidently thought him, with his deeply tanned skin, his alligator teeth and 'passport stick', a cannibal chief. An attempt was made on his life by a native leader who coveted his tomahawk; but Rougemont escaped by leaving his tent, which on his return in the morning was pierced by spears. He discovered a gibbering white imbecile, who in a lucid moment turned out to be the lost Gibson of the Giles Expedition of 1874. (He died too.) Rougemont challenged a jealous medicine-man to a duel of magic, privily draining a nest of snakes of their venom and then allowing them to bite him all over in public – a feat the witch-doctor was unwilling to copy. He finally rejoined civilization at Coolgardie, pretending to be a lost gold prospector. After a brief stay in New Zealand he landed in London in March 1898.

*   *   *   *   *

De Rougemont's adventures, which the *Wide World Magazine* began publishing in August 1898, continued through several issues; but in 1899 George Newnes collected the adventures into a single, attractively bound volume, to which William G. Fitz-Gerald, Editor of the *Wide World Magazine*, contributed a preface about his first meeting with Rougemont:

It was about four in the afternoon of a late spring day when a timid tap came at my door, and a man of striking appearance entered. Without a word he handed me a note from my friend Mr. J. Henniker Heaton, M.P., whom, it appeared, he had seen two or three times at the Carlton Club. My visitor explained that every one in Sydney had advised him to seek out the well-known M.P. on arrival in London.

I questioned the man. He said he had a remarkable story to tell – thirty years among the cannibals of unexplored Australia. His manner was quiet and courteous and his accent foreign. Adroit traps set for him in conversation only resulted in the absolute conviction that he was speaking the truth. . . . My shorthand writer commenced taking down the story next day. . . .

'He was hurled right over my head.'

The editor's preface to the first of Rougemont's series stated that Rougemont 'has already appeared before such eminent geographical experts as Dr J. Scott-Keltie and Dr Hugh R. Mill, who have heard his story and checked it by means of their unrivalled collection of latest reports, charts and works of travel. These well-known experts are quite satisfied that not only is M. de Rougemont's narrative perfectly accurate, but that it is of the very highest scientific value. . . .'

For one at least of these scientific experts, his involvement in the Rougemont affair was a slur from which his reputation never fully recovered – a millstone for Dr Mill, the meteorologist and oceanographer to whom we owe the introduction of sub-surface contours on the lakes shown on British Ordnance Survey maps. In 1898 he was Recorder of the Geographical Association. In his *Autobiography*, published in 1951, he wrote:

The most remarkable event in my recordership was certainly a paper read by a mendacious rascal, Louis de Rougemont, regarding his adventures in Australia. A highly coloured version of these had appeared in the *Wide World Magazine*, the editor of which had asked Keltie and me to test the truth of de Rougemont's statement that he had been in Australia, which we were able to do. After his paper had been accepted by the Sectional Committee, facts came to my knowledge which led me to propose that it should not be read; but the paper was allowed to go forward by a majority and was listened to by a very crowded house, the comments made upon it suggesting that it was a great exaggeration of real experiences. Subsequent discussion in the *Daily Chronicle* discredited the author, and brought undeserved aspersions on the Association and its officers. A legend that Keltie and I had been partners in deception is revived periodically in spite of successive vindications of our good faith.

It was after five instalments of his adventures had appeared that Rougemont was invited by the British Association for the Advancement of Science to give two lectures at the September meeting held in Bristol. On September 9 he addressed the Anthropological Section on 'The Natives of North-West Aus-tralia' and on the 12th he spoke to the Geographical Section on 'Twenty-Eight Years in Australia'. On each occasion an overflow audience stood on ladders outside the hall and peered in at the performance. There were several sceptics, notably the editor of the *London Chronicle*, who scented a scoop and put several reporters on the task of finding out the truth.

It took them under a month. On October 7 screaming headlines in the *Chronicle* asked: 'Who is de Rougemont?' and answered, 'Well, his name is not Louis de Rougemont. It is Henri Louis

'Some of the blacks intercepted us'

Grin!' And then the half-seedy, half-romantic story unfolded.
Grin had been born in 1847 by the Lake of Neuchâtel in the
village of Gresset, his parents being Swiss peasants, who lived in
a cottage called La Pelouse (The Lawn). Until sixteen he worked
as a farmer's boy; then he obtained work as a footman to the
actress Fanny Kemble, with whom he toured Europe and
America for seven years. With her, he learnt fluent English. In
1870 he left Fanny Kemble to become a valet to M. Mieville, a

Swiss banker living in London. He stayed with the Mieville family until 1874. That year, he arrived in Australia as butler to the new governor of the colony, Sir William Robinson. When pouring out wine for the governer's guests, Grin often heard stories of great explorers, such as Colonel Egerton Warburton who had made an epic journey across the desert from Alice Springs to Roebourne, or John Forrest, who in December 1874 returned to Perth after crossing Central Australia from Perth to the Overland Telegraph Line, and thence to Adelaide. Grin was inspired by these stories, and after five months in Robinson's service, resigned and prepared for a life of adventure. At Schubert's boarding house in Fremantle he found a gullible old gentleman named Coulson, who put up the money to buy a ten-ton cutter, *Ada*, of which Grin became master in June 1875. He made several pearling trips near Broome, but towards the end of 1876 he failed to return one day, and the *Ada* was officially posted as missing in February 1877. Grin, meanwhile, was sailing up the coast of Western Australia, past the north-west Cape, past Dampier's Archipelago, past Cape Londonderry, putting into La Crosse Island at the mouth of Cambridge Gulf for wood, water, and high jinks with the natives. Some months later the *Ada* was found by the Cooktown pilot boat, windbound north of Cape Bedford, thirty miles out of Cooktown. She had travelled half-way round Australia, 3,000 miles from Fremantle. Only Grin was aboard; he reported that he had been attacked by natives and his companions speared. There was no way of checking the story. In his subsequent career, Grin was a photographer in Port Douglas in the gold-rush days, where in the pubs he heard stories of Jemmy Morrill, the white castaway who lived seventeen years with the natives; he became a dishwasher at Webber's Post Office Hotel, Sydney, in 1880; he went pearl-diving in the Gulf of Carpentaria, was wrecked and lost everything; he invented a new process of enamelling photographs, but could raise no capital for a business, so became a photographer's canvasser.

In 1882 he married Elizabeth Jane Ravenscroft, an assistant in a fancy-goods store in Sydney. For fifteen years the couple lived precariously in Station Street, Newtown, Sydney, Grin taking jobs as waiter, real estate salesman, photograph tinter, and

inventor of a new brass diving suit in which a Danish diver was
drowned when it was tested outside Sydney Heads. In 1896, the
year of this catastrophe, Grin left his wife and children and
crossed the Tasman. Among his few personal effects was a part
of the diary of Harry Stockdale, the Centralian explorer, whom
Grin had met in a Newtown café: Stockdale's account was to be
the basis of much of his own. In New Zealand he became a
spiritualist for a time; but in March 1898, the gaunt Swiss ex-
butler with the seamed face arrived in London as a steward on
the SS *Waikato* from New Zealand. He found lodgings in Soho
and spent three months in the British Museum studying Australian and South Sea literature.

In the late spring of 1898 a French nobleman, Count Louis de
Rougemont (the name was pillaged from a tedious scriptural
writer, one of whose books is in the British Museum library),
called at the Carlton Club, London, and presented his card to
Mr J. Henniker Heaton, M.P. for Canterbury, who had lived in
Australia for many years and had published, in 1879, the *Australian
Dictionary of Dates and Men of the Time*. From Henniker Heaton, as
we have seen, Rougemont obtained his introduction to the
editor of the *Wide World*.

Rougemont's (or Grin's) fame as an impostor was far greater
than his fame as a *bona fide* explorer: the public always enjoys a
good fake more than the real thing, especially if some experts are
discomfited. The *Daily Chronicle* revelations were reprinted as a
book with gleeful illustrations by Phil May – who had also worked
in Australia and come to England to make his fortune. Rougemont's effigy was added to Madame Tussaud's. He revisited
Sydney, where he was advertised as 'the greatest liar on earth'.
The grizzled adventurer was received with 'a hail of rude inter-
jections'. According to Frank Clure's amusing biography of Grin
(1945) he died in the Infirmary of the Kensington Workhouse,
London, on June 9, 1921.

A sensational failure, one might think; but Rougemont's
achievements should not be discounted. First, he was one of the
great impostors of history, in the same rogues' gallery as Lambert
Simnel, Perkin Warbeck, Chatterton, Ossian, the Tichborne
Claimant, Thomas Wise, Baron Munchausen and the tailors of

the Emperor's New Clothes. Secondly, he was a superb writer of fiction, who can bear comparison with the contemporary Rider Haggard and even with Defoe himself. Verisimilitude is in general adeptly sustained, and occasionally the narrative rises to a pitch of comic invention which neither Defoe nor Haggard can rival; for example, when Rougemont, anxious to retrieve the prestige lost by telling the natives that his ruler is a woman, draws on a rockface a giant portrait of Queen Victoria to impress them:

. . . I commenced to draw in bold, sweeping outline, what I venture to describe as the most extraordinary portrait of Queen Victoria on record. The figure, which was in profile, was perhaps seven or eight feet high. . . . Of course, the figure had to be respresented entirely without clothing, otherwise the blacks would simply have been puzzled. . . . The crown was composed of rare feathers such as only a redoubtable and cunning hunter could obtain; and it included feathers of the lyre-bird and emu. The sceptre was a supendous gnarled waddy or club, such as could be used with fearful execution amongst one's enemies. The nose was very large, because this among the blacks indicates great endurance; whilst the biceps were ab-normally developed. In fact, I gave Her Majesty as much muscle as would serve for half-a-dozen professional pugilists or 'strong men'. The stomach was much distended . . . as the stomach is practically the greatest deity these savages know, and as food is often very hard to obtain, they argue that a person with a very full stomach must necessarily be a daring and skilful hunter, otherwise he would not be able to get much food to put into it. . . .

Finally, Rougemont's account probably suggested to Sir James Barrie the name for Peter Pan's country: Rougemont wrote, 'I, a white man, was alone among the blacks in the terrible land of "Never Never" – as the Australians call their *terra incognita*.'

It is surprising that no film has ever been made of Rougemont's adventures, which would be every bit as exciting on the screen as *Treasure Island*, *She* or *Mutiny on the Bounty*. Kangaroo millionaires and Zürich gnomes should vie in putting up money for such a venture: it would do honour to a hero of both nations who, at least in his own eyes, ranked somewhere between Ned Kelly and William Tell.

The illustrations by A. Pearse are from the original publication in the *Wide World Magazine*.

The School-Leaver

BY RONALD BLYTHE

THERE WAS a Greek called Mimnermus whose poems turned mourning into an amorous activity. So, in their way, did the Victorians. Ourselves, in contrast, have declared it a disease and something to get out of our systems as quickly as possible. Obituary notices are quite authoritarian about it. Don't waste your money on flowers; don't come to the funeral; don't write letters or, if you do, expect two lines in a newspaper by way of an answer. Give no expression to your lament: if you do we shall take you to the doctor. Only the *In Memoriam* column of the national and provincial press occasionally provides words which allow the old, sweetly indulgent sadness to have its satisfying fling.

The words are often those written by a twenty-two-year-old Eton master as an aid to a Greek textbook his class was studying in 1845, an eight-line poem called 'Heraclitus'. Over the last century few anthologies have been without it. Neither the class of '45 nor the countless people who have since reprinted it to sum up their loss are likely to have realized that behind its use, as an exercise or as a deliciously gloomy farewell, it encapsulates the dilemma of William Johnson's (its author) own life, and incorporates an extraordinary amount of information about the problem of parting in the classical world.

It will be necessary to quote the poem.

> They told me, Heraclitus, they told me you were dead,
> They brought me bitter news to hear and bitter tears to shed.
> I wept, as I remember'd, how often you and I
> Had tired the sun with talking and sent him down the sky.
>
> And now that thou art lying, my dear old Carian guest,
> A handful of grey ashes, long, long ago at rest,
> Still are thy pleasant voices, thy nightingales, awake;
> For Death, he taketh all away, but them he cannot take.

Who is speaking? It is a schoolmaster in Alexandria, Calli-machus, who later became a poet and an historian. William

Johnson was a poet, and when he had given up teaching – or when teaching gave him up – he wrote *A Guide to Modern English History*. Who was Heraclitus? He was Callimachus's great pupil-friend, a stylish poet who lived faraway in the lovely seaside city of Halicarnassus, the capital of Caria, a country named after Car, a king who predicted the future by the flight of birds. When he was a schoolmaster at Eton William Johnson, a subversive, magical kind of male Miss Jean Brodie, set out to breed a special sort of individual for the proconsulates and thrones of the British Empire. 'My pigeons go forth', he wrote, 'and bring back little sprays from the olive tree of truth.' But when, as must happen after the usual number of terms, the birds left the nest for good, he was desolated. In his private rooms, where his real teaching was done, rather than in Upper School, where several masters and hundreds of boys battled it out, the pleasant voices of his patrician band continued to fill his ears long after their owners had soared off to varsity or colony. He tried to be brave – 'I do not pity you for going away, it is your profession' – but he never got used to it. The elegy we borrow for the obituary column was composed for the inevitable parting between the teacher and the taught. While the rest of Victorian Eton thundered through the paces of what was hopefully described as a classical education, Johnson, with his unerringly chosen few, let in the disturbing flow of real Hellenism.

> Now lift the lid a moment: now Dorian shepherd speak:
> Two minds shall flow together, the English and the Greek.

Its long-term effect on the future ruling caste of Pollocks, Luxmoores, Roseberys, Halifaxes, Lytteltons, etc., was subtle but sure, and the nineteenth century is just that bit more compli-cated because of it. After the fall – for Brodies and Johnsons always come a cropper – the favourites of this Eton Socrates refused to abandon him and took to migrating to his exile in Devon, and when he died and was laid to rest in the composite arms of Jesus and Jupiter in Hampstead churchyard they clubbed together to publish his *Letters and Journals*. Issued in 1897 and never reprinted, it is one of the most beautiful and intriguing private documents of the Victorian age, and is only equalled by Kilvert's *Diary*. Before looking more closely at the man who wrote it, it is only fair to add that physical death, as well as death by parting, is present in *Heraclitus*. For one of the kings of Caria was Mausolus whose wife so adored him that when he died she ate his ashes and then created a ravishing building in his memory which became one of the Seven Wonders of the World – the Mausoleum. As with civilized, heartfelt, permissible mourning, metaphor and the actual, the welcome and the unbearable, 'the handful of grey ashes' and the 'nightingales' have their place.

William Johnson was born in 1823, the son of a Devonshire squire and a great-niece of Sir Joshua Reynolds. When he was ten he was sent as a pupil to Eton. The school was then entering upon the final years of the extraordinary reign of Dr Keate, the great flagellant headmaster whose brutalizing effect on society in the long term must have been incalculable. Like most monsters, he has become a legend and his licensed sadism a joke. In later life Johnson did his best to make out a case for Keate's passion for birching naked children, which he often did – a dozen or more at a time.

> To fit Keate into English history, I should like to point out how our good grandsires were forced to do honour to ferocity, because of the Mutinies. The very time of Keate's beginning work as an assistant is also the mutiny time, when the splendid courage of Jervis, Earl St Vincent, saved the country. . . . For some years our sea-captains were tempted into terrible fierceness. [Naval officers] had to be terrible when there were real dangers to the Commonwealth; and the squires, who knew how hard it was to rule the peasants, wished no doubt to have their beefy brats coerced sharply.

This was the devil's advocacy of an old man. No one when young did more to counteract the cruelty and philistinism of England's most important public school, and thus England's public life, than this eccentric, fastidious master, who was to spend some thirty-seven years there and to resurrect amongst its loutish customs and tepid scholarship the flame of true learning. Not that William Johnson was before his time. He was the personification of the high-mindedness of his age, a Burne-Jones knight with a pure face in a darkening garden, his sexuality faintly smudged yet present, his motto made indecipherable by rampaging undergrowth.

Naturally he loved war. Thermopylae and the Charge of the Light Brigade, Cannae and Majuba, were they not flashes of the same glory? The guards thrilled him; 'No girl has a steadier "scarlet fever" than I.' He liked to observe 'romantic, chivalrous friendships forming under my eye' but, alas for his ease of heart, such friendships never had the sense to know where to stop. They should have shone like Pre-Raphaelite daisies about his armoured feet, instead of which they pressed in upon his susceptible shield, his Anglican Hellenism, like creeper on a rectory, obliterating its principles. All the same, he told himself that 'age has for youth a natural priesthood' and encouraged many confessions.

Prevented by poor sight from playing ball games, Johnson took to the river. His *Journal*, which he kept only during the holidays, so that it abounds with recreational impulses which detach him from the immediate 'excitement' of Eton, his word for describing the effect which the school had for him, has limpid river scenes flowing through it. His rivers were the Cam, the Torridge and, of course, the Thames. Boating, idling, rowing, arranging floating parties, roused him to familiar heights of English ecstasie. Surrounded by his Favoured Ones, or sometimes simply little Devonshire girls whom he ferried through sedge and loosestrife in search of kingfishers, his own beaky head aslant to breathe in every ounce of the dank scent released by the oars, Johnson would continue to cast his academic spell. By mid-life he had become aware that conventional schoolmastering and himself were at odds and that 'Nature never intended me for a disciplinarian, much less a martinet, rather for a 'guerrillero'. But in 1868, when he wrote the following perfect account of a Victorian summer evening, the rapids were approaching.

Election Saturday, July 25. [The day on which the 'Tugs' or Collegers for the year were elected.] I went at 8.15 in the glow of sunset up the river to meet the boats coming down. I met swarms and lines of boys coming down. For the most part I escaped them by keeping to the right, favoured by the twilight, but some of them saw me; however I went on like a ghost, silent, looking at no one, bent only on keeping my freedom, my right to go against the stream, my right to see the pretty sight of the long boats and their curtseying flags come out of locks in the light that suits my eyes; all the vulgarity of their singing did not kill the beauty of their movements. The band – a vile band – played the old 4th of June tune which Scott Holland used to like. There was a half moon on the right, queening it in spite of rowdies; and I saw a dear form in a light blue coat standing up to take the Henley crew through the crowd of inferior boats. I stood alone, watching, listening, rehearsing the part of a discharged usher. They got clear of each other, and with my glasses I followed their curves of movement far down the dear river. I thought of young men quartered in Indian hill-forts, droning in twos or singly through a steaming night, miserably remembering their last row at Eton, pining and craving for lost youthfulness. . . . Presently I was in absolute solitude, sitting on a well-known stile, watching the rockets cross the breadth of South Meadow and Brocas. Now and then a fixed firework blazed up so as to show what I knew to be a mass of people looking on from the bank, and their cheers were transfigured into pure joy at that distance. Clewer Tower in the background; behind a spiritual after-glow; on my right lady moon; wind up stream, letting the little meteors fall slowly, well above the crowd.

Five years earlier there had been a night when he couldn't sleep because 'a half-humorous, half-sentimental boating-song for the 4th June' kept going round and round in his head. Eventually, he fixed it to paper and sent it to Algernon Drummond, an atypical member of the Anointed Ones, being artistic and dreamy and not proconsular material, a boy who liked sitting on window-seats listening to barrel organs playing *Ah che la morte* from *Trovatore*, but who, nonetheless, was now stationed in Lahore with the Rifle Brigade. Drummond set it to music and returned it. The song swept the College, a refined hand eventually substituting 'bodies' for 'bellies' in the last line.

> Jolly boating weather
>   And a hay harvest breeze,
> Blade on the feather
>   Shade off the trees,
> Swing, swing, together,
>   With your bellies between your knees.
>
> CHORUS
> Skirting past the rushes,
>   Ruffling o'er the weeds
> Where the lock stream gushes
>   Where the cygnet feeds.

Let us see how the wine-glass flushes
At supper on Boveney meads, etc.

The decade surrounding this celebration of the river was the summit and perfection of Johnson's existence. Under Dr Hawtrey, flogger Keate's dandiacal successor, the College's loutishness had been stamped on and the meaningless treadmill of the Greek and Latin authors turned to enlightened use. Dr Hawtrey, whose physical hideousness was unforgettably mounted in a luxurious setting of scent, jewels and fine clothes, recognized in 'Billy' Johnson a sparkling rill from the true Platonic stream. Moreover, the boys loved him to cult-like excess, not only the inner circle of those well-bred spirits being trained to take over the Empire, but boys anywhere and everywhere. His primers – one was called *Noces* (Nuts) – were less like introductions to Latin than keys to dangerous living. His curious and enchanting personality impregnated the chalky air with heresy. Some got the liberating drift of it with an understanding which would later challenge the set rules of society, others, like Oscar Browning, would be confirmed in their faith that the world was an orchid house, or should be. So the terms ran on. Virgil and the Dorian shepherds were made so real that they might have been resident in nearby still-idyllic Slough, Queen Victoria was put out of court by eighteenth-century republicanism, dreams of Christian unity were frustrated by the Romans' apparent inability to walk in procession without rollicking, and a religious adoration of the English countryside filled a chronically bursting heart. Sometimes it was all too beautiful and he would tell a disciple, 'You are born into an age which, as far as England is concerned, has no serious grievances to be redressed. The battle of justice has been won; you live amongst refined people.' But all too often the glory of patrician adolescence was in itself forbidding and it 'was hard for an elderly man, encumbered with vanity, mannerism and authority to approach', and then the reek of mortality would creep along the Thames Valley.

The avenging angel struck at Easter 1872. The wonder was that Dr Hornby, the new headmaster who had succeeded Dr Hawtrey, was capable of so positive an action, for he was inertia personified.

Yet his energy on this occasion was prodigious and in a matter of hours he not only turned Johnson out of the paradise he had enjoyed, man and boy, for nearly forty years, but seems to have set in motion all the machinery for making him a non-person in the Soviet sense. His name was ripped from the records and obliterated on the very primers which he had written. He had uttered himself (*Ephaphtha*) too explicitly in a letter to a neophyte, it could have been. Or had shown himself too consumed with work and purpose when the dull old ex-athlete Hornby just wanted to jog along. It would be Oscar Browning's turn next.

Back in Devonshire, Johnson briefly 'meditated the ceremony of dying' then was overcome by another thought – he had left school! He was free. Telling himself that he was no older than Columbus was when he had ventured into a new hemisphere, he began to make plans. Could he not go to India and worship the Union Jack or, and here he really would show his intrepidity, might he not explore 'the headlands and bays of that *terra incognita*, girlhood . . .?' The prospect before him became so extraordinary that he set-to to bury his old life. He resigned his Fellowship at King's College, Cambridge, and changed his name to Cory. No more the agony of those earlier relationships.

I told M. to-night that tragic heartrending story of the two brothers who crossed and met and touched hands in the dark, going by train across Egypt, the one to India, the other from India, after years of separation. No Greek, no Arab could imagine the heroic flush and throb of such an interchange of Christian names in the midnight. Will they in the ages to come say of us, 'Those poor Englishmen whom Newman stirred so deeply could not conceive our emotions?' Love and part. Is it for this we are made? Strain tight then, whilst you may yet embrace, poor mortals. . . .

But at the same time, in his fiftieth year, he had been hurt beyond denial. 'I go under a tunnel . . . I break my heart every day . . . I have undergone a very strange wounding.' For six years he balanced between the edge of his old existence and the brink of the new, during which time the *terra incognita* was cautiously spied upon. Girls played soft cricket against a background of weigelia, guelder roses, golden feather, lilacs, broom and azaleas. Girls piled up in flowery heaps in the boat shooting down the swift Torridge. They were bright inside as well as out, and their modulated lady voices winding their way round Homer and Livy obliged him to admit that 'the two undying evergreen languages have been for me made beautiful by this after-growth of girl-hood'.

In August 1878, when he was fifty-six and she was twenty, he married Miss Rosa Caroline de Carteret Guille, one of the many children of the local rector, to the scandal of the village and the puzzlement of all those who could not accept her statement, 'I always wanted to marry an *old*, clever man'. The sibilance in the word Mrs being unendurable, he insisted on her being addressed as Madame. For the early part of their life together they set up house in Madeira, where the visiting sailors devoured her with their hungry eyes and rich *émigré* consumptives stared sadly at her bursting health. Although a son, Andrew, arrived, Johnson-Cory could never bear to write or say 'my wife'. 'We are Philemon and Baucis, not Jack Spratt and his wife.' Reading her *Tom Sawyer*, playing with Andrew, musing on his bisexuality, keeping in touch with his élite, now carrying his quirkily different message to embassy and regiment, bench and Parliament, he stuck it out until he realized that both he and Madame were perishing from listlessness. For her, Madeira was a 'dying place'; for him it was the continuation of being psychically and socially dislocated.

In 1882 he got one of the Theban band to do a deal with young Baron von Hügel for his rather boring house in Hampstead, and, with the bird-like swoop which accompanied all his major decisions, Mr Cory arrived home to his beloved England. His brother, who had also changed his name (from Johnson to Furse in order to inherit a country property), had a son, Charles Furse, the charming, consumptive artist, who, when he was twenty-three, painted a remarkably understanding portrait of the ageing Johnson-Cory-Callimachus. It shows him head in hand, profile in darkness, hair and neck still catching the light and vitality from which his countenance shrinks. A man of shadows and skull-exploding memory. While sitting for it, balanced on a hard chair in the Hampstead silence (he and Baron von Hügel between them had managed to divert a scheme for running trams through the Heath), Cory whistled *Vedrai carina* and *Chefarò*, and admired the artist's 'energy, tact and good nature'.

The unknown land of girlhood was now opened up – had been for nearly two decades. Studious females filled the house, their eyes occasionally wandering from Lucretius to 'phots' of beautiful Etonians at the wicket or at the oar. They were the 'girls of the Newnham age, I mean the age of Melissa' and the pleasure he found in them was never very short of miraculous. Madame, still little more than a girl herself, was less studious and, when death came to her old, clever man in June 1892, went to where he would never have expected to find her, a beauty shop in Bond Street. And from thence, via business calamity, to obscurity with a French husband. When old, Callimachus had also married a young girl. Her name was Nanno, and nobody knew what became of her either.

From William Johnson's Cambridge Journal, April 1845:

And this too will pass away – this second boyhood now flourishing in King's, this interest in the state of my sinews and wind. All our crew will be broken up, and I shall be thinking that I have lost forever some spring of existence; and yet, if I live at all, I have no doubt that I shall hit upon something else. . . .

I think death is all the more terrible the less we talk about it – for instance, it never seems a more awful thing to me than when I think of it in connexion with one of those youthful associates (such as members of our boat crew), with whom one never by any chance speaks of dying as a thing they have anything to do with *personally*. . . .

I am going into an abyss of drudgery – I must float upon the hope of some success in perhaps one pupil out of fifty – the hope that before my time is out I may rejoice in having turned out . . . one brave soldier or one wise historian or one generous legislator or one patient missionary. . . . I do distinctly feel that if I have a gift it is the power of gaining influence over the minds of people more ignorant than myself. . . .

> *I live, I am old, I return to the ground:*
> *Blow trumpets, and still I can dream to the sound.*

Hellgate, Cripplegate, and Newgate

BY CHARLES NEILSON GATTEY

I N 1873 A MAN STOOD in the foyer of London's Haymarket
Theatre staring at an old play-bill recording the entertainment presented more than eighty years previously at the
7th Earl of Barrymore's private theatre in Savile Row. 'That is
what I shall call myself in future,' said the stage-struck Herbert
Blythe, son of a judge, who thereupon changed his name to
Maurice Barrymore. It was thus, according to the future 'Royal
Family of Broadway', that they acquired their surname. John
Barrymore, Blythe's son, claimed that the judge's wife was in
some way descended from the 7th Earl, but this is unlikely
though she may well have been from his successor.

The title had been conferred by Charles I on a dare-devil Irish-
man, David Barry, Viscount Buttevant, as a reward for military
services. His descendant, the debonair and dissipated 6th Earl,
died young when starting to gamble away the fortune derived
from his 140,000 acres in County Cork. Towards the end of his
short life he was inclined to employ doubtful practices to win his
wagers. Once he visited a tavern near Charing Cross and ordered
dinner in a private room. After the meal he asked not to be
disturbed. Then the waiter from below heard bumps and thuds
as if furniture was being moved, and on investigation found
tables and chairs dragged out on to the landing. He peeped
through the keyhole and saw the Earl on his knees, carefully
covering the floor with rows of playing cards.

A few days later the Earl returned with his friends and had
dinner served in the same room, after which he challenged his
guests to bet £500 that he could guess more accurately than any
of them how many cards would cover the floor. The wager was
accepted and, of course, he won.

The raffish peer left four children who were destined to have
sobriquets bestowed upon them by 'Prinny'. Sprightly Caroline,

A Hellgate Black...   A Newgate Scrub   A Cripplegate Monster

LES TROIS MAGOTS.

A satirical engraving by James Gillray

the first-born, he dubbed 'Billingsgate' because of her piquant vocabulary. Richard, her eldest brother, was somewhat harshly labelled 'Hellgate'. Henry, on account of his club-foot, became 'Cripplegate', and Augustus 'Newgate' after the only prison in which he had not resided. The first three were all born on dates in the middle of August and the youngest who arrived in the world in July was named after the month in which he should have appeared.

Richard Barry lost his father in 1772 when he was three, and his mother when eleven. Finding him unruly and precocious, she had him brought up by a kindly parson named Tickell at Wargrave by the Thames. Both tutor and pupil became fond of each other, though the former recorded that his charge's 'impatient volatility rendered him inflexible to remonstrances and left no hopes of success, but from such manual chastisement as the philosophic mind rejects and reason revolts at'. In view of this, Richard's grandmother sent him to Eton three years after the Countess's death, indulgently giving him at the same time £1,000 as pocket money.

Three months later the old lady herself died, which left the children virtually without anyone to control them. Dr Davies, the Headmaster at Eton, was rarely sober, and was mostly away roistering in London. Richard caught gambling fever at fifteen and went to Newmarket and backed a winner. The bookmaker handed him a wad of notes, fifty pounds short of the correct thousand guineas, confident that this slight, inexperienced boy would not count what he was given. But he did, proving that he was no fool. 'I want another fifty,' he demanded, and without a word the man parted with the money.

Beginner's luck made the young Earl decide that he would own his own stud when he grew up. At Eton he also became a practical joker, and with Henry and Augustus would roam the countryside after midnight changing inn and road signs so that travellers went astray. For some such escapade, that led to discovery, he was asked to leave the College when in his eighteenth year. Impatient not to have to await the reaching of his majority before beginning to spend his fortune, he obtained advances through a moneylender, 'Black Jack', who took charge of his finances for a time and was known as his nurse.

This enabled Richard to set up a splendid establishment. When he took the field with his pack of hounds and his faultlessly horsed retinue, including four negroes in liveries of scarlet and silver, expertly sounding French horns, people said it was like the *chasse* of Louis XIV. Anthony Pasquin, the poet and playwright, whom he employed as his amanuensis, wrote that he was a bold rider, but not a uniformly bold hunter. He would sometimes retreat from leaps which his companions had already made. 'I have seen him plunge with his horse into the Thames and swim to the other side; and a few days after hesitate to fly over a small hedge.'

In 1787 Barrymore formed a stud. He began by purchasing a

filly 'Yarico', which won its first race. As an owner he showed himself to be a shrewd observer of form with remarkable judgement in handicapping horses. He had a flair for doing the right thing and made money on the turf. With a view to popularizing his blue and yellow racing colours he dressed his coachman and footman in them, but they soon gave notice, complaining that the 'lower orders' mistook them for escaped convicts, so he had to agree to clothe them normally.

According to Pasquin, the Earl himself was 'the best coachman in the kingdom'. He had frequently been conveyed in his phaeton and four over cross-roads in the country when it was so dark that they could scarcely perceive the leaders. Sometimes Richard hired a mail coach and horses. 'I once saw a party set off for Newmarket in the middle of the night with himself on the coach-box.' Barrymore's frolicsome nature, however, got the better of him on occasion. When he drove from London to Wargrave in the small hours, and passed through a narrow road at Colnbrook, he would whip right and left, cracking the window panes. He called this 'fanning the day-lights'.

Life for him at Wargrave was one long house party. His home there was small, so he constructed a two-storeyed annexe, known as the 'upper and lower barracks' where rows of hammocks hung ready for those who wanted to snatch some sleep. No one was allowed to retire till 5 a.m.

Barrymore was an excellent chef, who enjoyed arraying himself in white hat and apron and preparing a superb supper for favourite companions. Though fond of having the bottle circulate freely at his table, and a provider of free Burgundy to all bargees passing on the river, he himself was not a deep drinker. A beef-steak and a pint of wine formed the whole of his dinner throughout most of the year. The reason for his preventing guests from retiring early was probably his sleeplessness. He was abnormal regarding his bedroom whether at home or elsewhere. His valet's first duty was to sew the sheets to the blankets so that no part of the latter touched his skin. Then the man had to cover every window with blankets, three or four thick, to shut out any light. If a fire were burning in the grate, it had to be extinguished and every glowing cinder removed.

Women played little part in his life and his only passion was for acting. Well over six foot tall, slim, a deft dancer, with a mobile, handsome face, thick curly hair, lively eyes, and a voice that could assume with conviction any accent from a courtly French to the slang of stable, prize-ring or thieves' kitchen, he had a gift for comedy that might have brought him fame had he become a professional. Whilst still at Eton he turned a barn at Wargrave into a theatre and presented Garrick's *Miss in her Teens* with himself as 'Flash', Henry and Augustus as 'Puff' and 'Fribble', and the village youth in the other parts. This was so well received by an audience of farmers and their wives that eighteen months later he employed Mr Cox, former carpenter to Covent Garden Theatre, to build him at a cost of £60,000 what was soon acknowledged to be the finest private theatre in the country.

The brothers and their sister, Caroline, who when required played the harpsichord, formed the nucleus of the company, together with friends, and were strengthened with guest professionals. If Barrymore lacked among the amateurs an actor or actress capable of undertaking an important part, he sent to London with offers of lavish fees and carte blanche as to wardrobe, and down came Mrs Goodall or Miss Richards or one of the actors from Drury Lane or Covent Garden. The famous clown, Delphini, from the latter theatre, joined him and remained as stage manager with his wife as housekeeper. As a result, productions were on so high a level that the county aristocracy packed the three performances given each week. Admission was free, but by invitation only.

As an extension, Richard added a circular room with a dome lit by coloured lamps, beneath which from a round sideboard cake, negus and all kinds of drink were dispensed gratis during the intervals to the audience by six menservants resplendent in scarlet and gold.

At dress rehearsals, Pasquin tells us, 'all the inferior people were admitted, such as servant maids, dairy wenches, shepherds and ploughboys – all the rows of the pit filled with red cloaks and smock frocks in chequered order looked like red and white cabbages arranged in Covent Garden market'. He adds that it amused Barrymore when not on the stage to listen from a side box to the remarks of 'these idealess, inane animals'. But if the Earl was contemptuous of the yokels, he had entirely different feelings for actors and actresses. Unlike most people of the period he had the highest regard for them. He once asked Pasquin if he did not think it extraordinary that actors were not more 'unequivocally admitted to the privileges of gentlemen, especially as it was imagined by the most critical individuals that it required a greater portion of combined merit to excel upon the stage than in any other professional department of life'.

Richard excelled when he and his friend, Captain Watken, played 'Archer' and 'Aimwell' in *The Beaux' Stratagem*, the gentlemen of broken fortune pretending to be servant and master. This character he changed afterwards for what became his favourite rôle, that of 'Scrub', the witty servant of all work to 'Squire Sullen', who thus summarizes his duties: 'Of a Monday I drive the coach, of a Tuesday I drive the plough, on Wednesday I follow the hounds, of Thursday I dun the tenants, on Friday I go to market, on Saturday I draw warrants and on Sunday I draw beer.'

It was not long before he grew dissatisfied with the smallness of his Wargrave theatre, and, uttering his pet phrase, 'Damn the expense', bought and refurbished Frantiocini's Marionette Theatre, 22–23 Savile Row, installing a new stage and enlarging the auditorium. It opened on July 22, 1790, with *The Beaux' Stratagem*. Mrs Goodall and his sister, Caroline, played the two female leads and he himself not only appeared as Scrub but at the end performed a *pas de Russe* with Delphini and was pronounced by the critics 'inimitable'. To entertain his patrons in style after performances he purchased a mansion in Piccadilly.

That September the Earl celebrated for five days at Wargrave his coming of age. For the first three nights there were consecutive performances of *The Follies of a Day* and a pantomime, *Robinson Crusoe*. In the one he took the part of a drunken gardener, and in the other a clown. The festivities ended with a masked ball attended by over five hundred persons of rank and fashion. The Prince of Wales travelled from Brighton on the day to be present, arriving at 4 p.m., and, after delighting the ladies by dancing with as many as he could, departed at dawn by coach for the races at York. The only contretemps was caused by the Earl's brothers, 'Cripplegate' and 'Newgate', who, disguised as barbers, shaved and powdered all who came their way.

Now, as Pasquin puts it, the Earl's munificence became ruinous. There would be aquatic fêtes and all would dine on some island between Henley and Reading – 'so inebriate the mimic crew that had not the venerable Thames been auspicious to the festival, half the assemblage would have been engulphed amid his mud'. The Earl increased his stud to thirty, buying the famous Chanticleer and Seagull from Charles James Fox. He founded one eccentric club after another, according to the whim of the moment. There was the 'Bothering', the 'Humbugging', the 'Warble' and the 'Two O'Clock', which entitled him to be regarded as the originator of the night club. He developed an enthusiasm for boxing and enlisted in his service a Cornish tin-man, Hooper, who though small beat men of much larger proportions. In February, 1790, Barrymore won £25,000 in bets when his pet beat 'Will of the Wisp' Watson. With cards, how-ever, he met disaster and once lost 2,800 guineas in one evening at *quinze*. The only time he won was through his opponent, Fox, wearing polished steel buttons on his coat which reflected the cards in his hand.

Having become friendly with the Prince of Wales, the Earl fell under the spell of Brighton and took a house there for the season. He was joined by his brothers and sister. 'Prinny' was at first amused by the men's practical jokes, but as these became wilder he regretted they had come to live near him. 'Hellgate', 'Cripplegate' and 'Newgate', as he now christened them, would promenade with Hooper disguised as a clergyman, and the bruiser would fly to their aid if somebody they purposely provoked rose to the bait and hit out at them.

One of the Earl's japes was to wear his housekeeper's gown and sing to guitar accompaniment *Ma Chère Amie* outside Mrs Fitzher-bert's house at 3 a.m., which angered the Prince, who was with her. Another incident shows him in a better light, as an animal-lover. Encountering a butcher on the Steine, who was inciting two dogs to fight, he ordered him to stop. The man was insolent. The altercation was followed by a fight which Barrymore won.

A coloured engraving of 1791

One prank nearly ended fatally when he had a footman strapped in a coffin so as to resemble a corpse, his face painted green, and then propped it against a tradesman's door. The knocker was hammered urgently, then Earl and friends raced to take cover. They saw the maid answering the summons shriek and faint, alarming her employer who, imagining they were being attacked by robbers, rushed out with blunderbuss and horse pistol which he discharged at the coffin, missing the footman's head by less than an inch.

By the age of twenty-four the Earl had spent over £300,000 and creditors were clamouring for payment. The crash came at last. His stud and stables, the Piccadilly mansion and the Savile Row theatre all were sold – no one would buy the one at Wargrave so it was demolished.

In those days an M.P. could not be arrested, so to insure against finding himself in a debtors' prison our Irish peer acquired a 'pocket' borough. Up till then only two women had been linked with him. There was the notorious Mie-Mie, 'Old Q''s natural daughter, who chased him in vain, and Antonietta who resembled Marie Antoinette. It was said that he first saw her on the stage in Paris and was so attracted by the rapid motions of her snowy legs that he engaged her for his theatres where she entertained him and his patrons by dancing between the acts. She then became joint-manager at Wargrave. But, discovering that he was undersexed, she took to drink and after she had fallen over dancing several times and finally through a trap-door, they parted.

Then, faced with his money troubles, he felt in need of feminine protection and decided to wed; but instead of choosing an heiress he married Charlotte Goulding, daughter of a sedan chairman. It is doubtful if the marriage was consummated, but she comforted him and tried in her gentle way to reform him, suggesting that he ought to do something positive with his life. As a result, to everybody's astonishment, he suddenly bought himself a commission in the Berkshire Regiment, feeling it was the right thing to do as war with France had broken out. But his military career proved a short one, for when escorting some prisoners from Rye to Deal his gun went off accidentally and the charge penetrated his brain. His body was taken in secret for burial at Wargrave to avoid the possibility of his creditors seizing it in the hope that friends would pay to give the deceased decent interment.

Henry Barry or 'Cripplegate' became the 8th Earl, and inherited his brother's extravagant tastes and habits but without the means to indulge them, though thanks to the rescue operation of Hammersley the banker he did eventually have an annual income of £10,000. Of aristocratic bearing despite his club-foot, pugnacious and quarrelsome, he was one of the founders of the 'Whip Club' and few could tool a four-in-hand like him. He also sported a much admired Stanhope in which he used to drive about town with a small boy beside him and thus originated the 'Tiger'. The first was Alexander Lee, son of the landlord of the 'Anti-Gallican' tavern.

The new Earl had a fine voice and would burst into song at every opportunity. He announced himself wherever he went by chanting the chorus of his favourite ditty – 'Chip Chow Cherry Chow-fol-lol-di-riddle-how'. His passion was card-playing.

Always in debt, he was constantly beset by bailiffs, and if their arrival at his house in Sackville Street interfered with a party, he would persuade them in return for a few coins to don some cast-off liveries and pretend to be his servants, so that the guests would not know their real identity.

He married Anna Coghlan of Waterford, who neither brought him money nor gave him any children. Her sister, however, wed an *émigré* who on the restoration of the Bourbons regained his French possessions and allowed his by then penurious brother-in-law and wife an apartment in his Paris mansion where they lived quietly. Once every month or so the Earl would pay his mistress in London a visit. This was Fanny Norton, whom he had bought from Hervey Aston and who had been handed over at a banquet arranged for the purpose, the lady being led in clothed in a single garment and with a string round her neck, the end of which was given by Aston to his lordship. She was then saluted as Lady Barrymore and shortly afterwards installed in a handsome house near Audley Square. After his death from apoplexy in 1823 she went from bad to worse, and she was found dead in the street in 1832 with an empty gin bottle in one hand and 2½d in the other.

Augustus Barry or 'Newgate' had pre-deceased the 8th Earl in 1811. He had joined the Berkshire Regiment about the same time as Richard, but had resigned his commission on his brother's unfortunate death so as to take holy orders, but no one would trust him with a living. Only Caroline or 'Billingsgate' remained of the quartet, and on Henry's death she assumed one of the family's titles and called herself Baroness de Barry without submitting her claim to this honour to the House of Lords. Little is known of the rest of her life, though some say she spent it attempting good works, affected by memories of the 8th Earl's last days. According to Captain Gronow, who knew him, he was then 'a martyr of the gout and other diseases; and on his deathbed he was haunted by the recollection of what he had been, and the thought of what he might have become: indeed, the last scene of his profligate life, when tortured by the inward reproaches of his accusing conscience, was harrowing in the extreme.' A perfect ending – for a Victorian cautionary tale.

A Day at the Derby

BY H. BERRY

The writer of this sketch, now an Old Age Pensioner, was a newsboy at Mitcham in Surrey during the First World War. This sketch describes going to the Derby in 1914, and it is printed exactly as it was written.

MUM LET ME GO to the Derby because WILL is having a new Bike made for him by FRED CANNON. CYCLE ENGINEER. PRAM REPAIRS. for 14/- for his birthday 1/- a week so he had to do my paper round at Dinner time and the Evening papers.

As soon as I got back from my morning round I set out for EPSOM DOWNS 5½ miles with my Dinner packed up in my RAMBLERS HAVERSACK that Mum made Unbleached Calico with a brass soldiers button ROYAL FUSILIERS with a bomb on it to do it up with. Bread and Dripping sandwiches thick and a BATEYS GINGER BEER bottle with HOME MADE LEMONADE in it that we make with Crystals and some broken biscuits. The biscuits got a bit more broken when I was going past ACME PRINTING WORKS. PRINTERS AND BOOKS BOUND because a Brake was going by and I called out Throw out your Mouldy Coppers and they did and I ran to pick them up then some boys ran out and charged me out of the way and the BATEYS Bottle got broken as well. I expect I will Cop it when Mum finds out because there is a ¼d on them bottles and my sandwiches got all WET but they were dry by dinner time.

I couldnt find any broken glass in them and I was too hungry to waste time looking for it much. I called out to more Brakes and Wagonettes and Traps with Plum pudding dogs running underneath them almost touching the horses hoofs but they didnt throw any Mouldy Coppers out. I suppose it would not make them laugh like it does when a lot of Kids push and Shove to get them.

When I got to WANDLE BRIDGE my feet were sweating hot and I wish I could lay down by the side of the road so that I could see all the traffic going by but all the grass and DANDELIONS and

MAY and DOG ROSES were all covered with dust which flies everywhere when the Motors go by.

So I went in a field that was Yellow with Buttercups up to your knees and laid down with my Plimsolls off and when I shut my eyes and listened I could still hear Horses Hooves on the road Concertina music. mouth organ music. a Cuckoo. people singing people laughing and a skylark high up in the sky. Then I heard a HUNTING HORN and just got to the gate when along come a 4 in Hand Coach with gentlemen with Grey TOP HATS and women with Big Hats and veils and they were all smiling like QUEEN ALEXANDRA and one man was blowing this long Hunting Horn.

I bet if I had called out MOULDIES I would have got some but I hadnt got any shoes on and had to go back for them. I bet they were real Lords and Ladies.

I saw a lot of Bikes go by and counted five Tandems and some Pearly Kings and Pearly Queens and their Kids in Donkey Carts then I went and paddled in the Wandle and there were 100s of Sticklebacks under the bridge and I found a newt and as I couldnt find a TIN or a Jamjar to put it in I left him in a hole that a Cows foot had made and covered him with leaves. I didnt like to put him in my Haversack with my sandwiches and it was too early to eat them.

Nearly every cottage on the road had got notices up CUT FLOWERS for SALE with all the Ss round the wrong way and one had TEAS with the S the wrong way round.

Along come a CART R. WHITES DELICIOUS MINERALS so I ran after it and hung on the Tailboard all the way to EPSOM DOWNS and no whip behind guvnor.

You could easily tell the way to the Races because there were crowds of People all going One Way and no one going the other way at all.

When I got on the Downs there were millions of People and there was a Roar of Noise like when you put Mums pink Shell to your ear only millions of times louder that she keeps on the overmantel with writing on it A PRESENT FROM SCARBOROUGH.

There were people selling all sorts of things like STILL LEMON-ADE. Slices of PINEAPPLE. Slices of Coconut. Race Cards.

Sarsapirilla. Wavers. and GENTS which was poles stuck in the ground and sacking nailed to it like a Tent but no roof on and the GIPSIES take a penny each from the Gents as they go in and it pongs. and Stalls with WHELKS and COCKLES in Vinegar and Rock.

I don't know what ever those men were doing because no one gave them any money but they just stood up on top of a box or on the roof of a Coach and one of them kept tapping the top of his head with a newspaper and pulling his ear and tapping his knee and putting his hand up quickly and all sorts of funny things like that and there were lots of them doing it but nobody laughed at them.

I asked a boy what they were doing and he said tictacsoppy but I don't know what he meant.

There were lots of men kept jumping up on to the Brakes and Traps and saying Mark your Card guvnor and sometimes people gave them Money and I watched a Gent all dressed up in a Grey Top Hat and best clothes like them on the top of the 4 in hand only he was selling little envelopes with A FORTUNE FOR 6d printed on them but he wasnt a real Lord or a proper Gent because I saw his boots and they were sort of worn out and filthy dusty.

One man who looked like a Jockey was letting people sit on a great big pair of scales all shining brass and he was weighing them with their CORRECT WEIGHT 1d.

Nearly everywhere you looked there was waste paper laying about and dust. orange peel and broken Wavers no good. and I kept looking but didnt find any Money.

Suddenly millions of people shouted out Theyre off and kept telling each other theyre off and then the Bookies started shouting quicker and quicker and their haversacks were full of money and all the people started shouting louder and quicker and nearly squealing out and then they stopped and some people RAN up to the Bookies for money and lots of people looked SAD and were tearing up their coloured Tickets and I picked up one that wasnt and it had got HAPPY JOE on it. That was the name that a Bookie had got painted on a Board where he was standing and I heard him say out loud to one man IT GIVES ME GREAT

PLEASURE to GIVE YOU ALL THIS MONEY SIR. I suppose thats why he is so Happy If you have got it to give away.

There were Donkey Rides and lots of things like WINKLES. TEAS. more SARSAPIRILLA. ICES. Beer Tents. Luncheons. A Professor PHRENOLOGIST which is reading the Bumps on your head who has got a Banner with a Map of your head on it. Coconut shies. Hoky poky. The Man with the Banner PREPARE TO MEET THY GOD who was at Mitcham Fair. an Artist doing PORTRAITS while you wait and another Artist who cuts out your Portrait in Black Paper and sticks it on a Card called SILHOUETTES. Sausage and Mash on a Cardboard plate and thousands of empty ones on the ground. FRUIT DRINKS 2d MONSTERS. in glass bottles with a glass marble in the spout which you press in before you can drink it. WAVERS. 3 Nigger Minstrels with Banjos only the black on their faces has made their Collars filthy. Lots of Gipsy kids begging for money. PHOTOS while you WAIT on bits of glass but Very Dark not very good. Sherbet Drinks. A man laying on the ground all tied up with iron Chains and his head in a sack and another man who came round with a Hat for the money who said his MATE would escape from the chains if he got threepence more in the Hat which he got and he did but I dont know how. A Salvation Army Band. MADAM M. PALMIST in a little tent.

I had my sandwiches there because there was a Water Fountain because my Still Lemonade all went when the BATEYS Bottle broke when I was going. I lined up for a drink out of the iron cup on a chain. I would have had two cups only the kid behind me put his finger over the water coming out of the tap and it sprayed every where and I got Sopping and everybody shouted and I got pushed off the Steps ERECTED by the ROYAL SOCIETY of CRUELTY TO ANIMALS as there was a Horse trough as well.

Its too hot to sleep and I've only got one SHEET over me in bed and thats too hot and my face is BURNING and my feet hurt and all them sparrows are kicking up such a row in the Ivy outside my window.

A
CABINET OF

Drawing for *Punch* by George du Maurier, 1888

CURIOSITIES

The Baroque of Salento

BY LAURENCE SCARFE

WITH PHOTOGRAPHS BY THE AUTHOR

THE HEEL of Italy, the Salento, must always have had about it something of the charms of a place where people on their way to somewhere else noted its attractiveness and decided to give it more than passing attention. For centuries this seems to have been the case and we find that the marauding nations, while pushing on to further adventures in the Levant, each left evidence of their sojourn in this fertile peninsula. The list of visitors is impressively nostalgic – across this neck of land came Romans, Byzantines and Longobards, Normans, Crusaders and Angevins, Aragonese and Spaniards. These thrusting characters stayed long enough to leave substantial architecture for the next wave to modify, so that today we are left with a somewhat confusing legacy of stylistic influences. In that delightful way which makes the mutation of architectural styles so intriguing, the confusion has been increased by local craftsmen, who, nearly always being natives of the place (slipping in their own ideas of design and actually wielding the hammers and chisels while their masters and patrons looked on), gave the sophisticated a touch of the unsophisticated. Thus it is that major styles become 'provincial', and provided the omens are good – as they seem to have been down there – produces an art that owes much to traditional culture sprung from the surrounding fields and quarries, often with an unabashed love of excessive ornament.

After travelling so far – and even today the Salento is well off the beaten track – it is an astonishing experience to discover the many towns and villages offering architectural delights quite unlike any in the rest of Italy. About Lecce, the capital of the province, there is an atmosphere of refined urbanity, hinting at a life of routine luxury for those who could afford to build grand private houses, a luxury absorbed by the Church in the gradual modification of its ancient buildings, bishops' palaces, seminaries and cloister gardens, and also in the embellishment of the city with its considerable display of municipal buildings and public monuments. While Lecce apparently never made much of a mark in history, its very remoteness at the end of Italy enabled it to enjoy an almost insular culture, tranquil and enclosed in its nature, reflecting the withdrawn characteristics of the Spanish life-style, and afterwards that of the aristocratic princi-palities of south Italy in the eighteenth century with their proud display of hierarchical pomp. Here was an artistic fusion, pursued over many generations, continuing the traditions of the Norman cathedrals and churches, and the tardy arrival of Renaissance ideas of secular elegance. In the seventeenth and eighteenth centuries there occurred a unique flowering, a boom period in building, partly Spanish in origin, modified by Italian influences which had percolated down from Naples and Rome, but modified still further – and decisively – by the genius of local artisans, who had preserved their craft techniques and expressed them in their love of ornamentation. The local masons and carvers put the finishing touches to imported styles and transformed them, less with scholarship than with *joie de vivre*. The results are happy and unpedantic, blithely transgressing canons of good taste. In fact the results are riotous, and have on occasion been referred to as 'orgiastic' by a number of writers from the North, more accus-tomed to *cinquecento* and *settecento* proprieties, the refinements of Tuscany, the heavy splendours of Rome.

The so-called Baroque of Lecce, while hinting here and there at the playful antics of Borromini but more definitely at the Neapolitan exuberance of Fanzago, is not strictly baroque. It can best be described as a local mannerism with roots in the medieval and Norman past. It is somewhat miraculous how the local carvers managed to incorporate artistic memories of things long past – the earlier love of the grotesque, the little monsters, sprites, gargoyles, weird animals and birds, the never-never plant forms, which riot everywhere and gaily infest and sprout on the pseudo-classical orders of the imported styles. The results are unique in the story of Italian Baroque architecture, and the conventions evolved are consistent and remarkably successful on façade after façade and in the many sumptuous interiors. They are proudly and self-confidently local – a kind of Baroque in holiday mood, a sculptural harvest festival in stone.

While the style is essentially sculptural, we ought not to ignore the school of local painters who helped matters along with equal enthusiasm in the scores of altar paintings and votive pictures, to be found, alas, sadly blackened by candle smoke and neglect. The cathedral at Gallipoli for instance seems to have almost as many paintings on its walls as the National Gallery in London! No doubt a few masterpieces will turn up one day, and the task can be recommended to some young art historian, so long as he has the time and stamina to delve in the byways of regional painting and the dust of local archives. The paintings are Matteo Preti-out-of-Caravaggio with a dash of Ribera, garlanded by amateur flower painters in sentimental mood. . . .

Stone carving, however, triumphs. The sculptures and architectural carvings are fresh and sharp: outdoors in the sunshine the effect is dazzlingly bright, indoors the whiteness persists, helped along by gold leaf . . . and also, sad to report, occasionally smothered by over-application of distemper. The facility of the carving grew naturally out of local materials. The peninsula provides an abundance of a marvellous limestone, golden and white, which when quarried is so soft that it can be carved into intricate shapes without breaking, and which, after a few years' exposure, hardens and retains the crispness in permanent form.

In Lecce the most extensively displayed double façades are those of the Governor's Palace and the Basilica of Santa Croce. That of the basilica was completed by the middle of the seventeenth century during the period of Spanish domination. It is a superimposition of enrichments on a Romanesque type façade, but which became a scenic masquerade of eagles, dragons, monkeys, Evangelists, Saints, Turks, swags, rosettes, variegated leaf mouldings, and urns, balusters, billets and balls. The total effect is delirious, and no Roman vulgarian at the Fall of the Empire or Victorian Gothic gargoyle-monger ever thought up such as this. Nevertheless, it is an architectural romp of the first order and quite original. The sculptor, as far as I can ascertain, was Cesare Penna (1607–80), a man of Lecce, with a confident imagination and a strong arm. The interior of the basilica is a pleasant contrast, flooded with light, of great dignity and calm, where the ornaments sprout with a more rhythmic order on capitals and arches (though still with the feeling of ostrich feathers) around the cupola, and on the very satisfactory flat ceiling of deeply carved and gilded coffers.

The sheer abandon and licence of Santa Croce must have put heart into those who came after – and accustomed the people of Lecce to expect something extra special for their money. The style proliferated in one building after another, though never with quite the same bravura. From about 1670–1710 followed a long series of churches and palaces in all parts of the city. In Lecce the architect Zimbalo (who, it is said, was nicknamed Lo Zingarello and was suspected of gypsy blood) was followed by his disciple Cino, and for twelve years they worked on the Duomo, completing it with a magnificent baroque belfry. It became part of a fine piazza along with the Bishop's Palace and the Seminary, lavish in detail but more sober in general conception, making this one of the finest squares in southern Italy. Nevertheless the Seminary by Cino has a massive portal and balcony which is perhaps the most elaborately treated of all the many balconies of Lecce, and in the courtyard is a central well with sculptured arch in the same blithesome spirit looking fine among trees. Also by Cino is the most harmonious church in Lecce, that of Sant' Irene, and just outside the city the façade of Santi Niccolò e Cataldo, one of the rare essays in stylistic amalgamation, in which he succeeded in marrying an existing Norman doorway of 1180 with a restrained use of Baroque details of 1716.

There are other towns with notable buildings – Galatone, Manduria, Francavilla Fontana, Nardo. . . . The latter is particularly charming, for whereas Lecce retains the dignity of white and pale grey stone and is sober in colour, in Nardo the great surprise is the use of colour-washed buildings. The effect is supplementary to the rich stonework, and whole streets and lanes and small squares are bathed in reflected light from red, rose-pink, yellow ochre or blue. There are many eighteenth-century balconies and doorways; a fine central piazza sporting a *guglia*, or central monument – an ornamental version of the Guglia di San Domenico in Naples, displayed against a town hall in Salentine rococo. The church of San Domenico in Nardo is once again a lavishly sculptured building, playfully grotesque, and on the outskirts is another monument named the Osanna, a pillared cupola with Mannerist Gothic and Baroque motifs.

For those with an appetite for the Baroque the Salento affords one cream-topped meal after another. The feast can continue for days, interspersed with lazy walks, gossip with the inhabitants (who can tell you nothing about their buildings), and much-needed siestas in the sweltering afternoons. The countryside, though said to be a paradise in spring, is impressively rocky and picturesquely dried up in summer. It is alive with butterflies and lizards and noisy with cicadas, and the sea is never far away. One village after another has its pride of buildings, far too numerous to recount here . . . palaces of noble families, cathedrals and chapels, and equally attractive simple houses.

Opposite: Detail of the lower half of the façade of the Chiesa di San Domenico, Nardo.

Opposite: The Guglia dell' Immacolata in the Piazza Salandra, and *above:* the Osanna, both in Nardo. The *guglia* is the principal monument in the main square, a richly carved tower with statuary, probably about 1650. The Osanna is a small temple with cupola and open columns, of earlier date.

Opposite: Two details from the Chiesa di Sant' Irene, the church of the Theatines in Lecce, early eighteenth century. The carving is inventive and bold. *Above:* a view of the upper section of the façade of the Basilica di Santa Croce, Lecce. The architects Zimbalo and Cesare Penna were the designers. Work continued enthusiastically till 1689.

Below: The façade of the Chiesa del Rosario, Lecce. Finished in 1752, attributed to Giuseppe Zimbalo and Giuseppe Cino. The details are celebratory and well mannered with personal varieties of capitals, discreetly witty. *Opposite:* Two further details from S. Irene, on the favourite theme of happy children.

Above: Cardiff Castle: the sunray chandelier, balcony and dome in the Summer Smoking Room. The metalwork was carried out for Burges by Hart, Son, Peard & Co. Opposite: sculpture by Thomas Nicholls in one of the porches of St Finbar's, Cork.

The Fabric of a Dream

BY OLIVE COOK

WITH PHOTOGRAPHS BY EDWIN SMITH

A SMALL BUT ATTRACTIVE MAN with a broad, noble fore-head, humorous, mild, short-sighted eyes and frizzy dundrearies framing a full, heavily moustached face, William Burges was a great talker, fond of company and addicted to jokes, both verbal and visual. He was known to his circle as Billy and concealed his erudition and deeply serious ambition behind such a display of high spirits that the general opinion of his friends was that expressed in D. G. Rossetti's limerick:

> There's a babyish party named Burges
> Who from infancy hardly emerges.
> If you had not been told
> He's disgracefully old
> You would offer a bull's eye to Burges.

[Continued on page 193

Above: Waltham Abbey, Essex. On the left: St Finbar's, Cork

Castell Coch, Cardiff Castle, the Clock Tower
Below: the courtyard, Castell Coch

Above, left: washstand of marble mosaic at Cardiff Castle, the basin inlaid with metal fish.
Above, right: Lord Bute's bedroom at Castell Coch
Below: Capital in the Summer Smoking Room, Cardiff Castle, carved by Thomas Nicholls, painted by Campbell, Smith and Campbell

Lady Bute's bedroom, Castell Coch

The Summer Smoking Room, Cardiff Castle

Looking into the Winter Smoking Room, Cardiff Castle

The impression of his not having completely grown up was reinforced by Burges's delight in play-acting. At home in his rooms in Buckingham Street he wore medieval dress; he had a vellum sketch book bound in purple velvet; and when he built his own house, The Towers, in Melbury Road, Kensington, he designed a day and a night nursery for it although at the time he was over fifty and a confirmed bachelor.

The sense of masquerade is certainly present in his work, but this is characteristic of most Victorian architecture; and there is nothing aesthetically immature about Burges's buildings. No artist of the period makes a more overwhelming impact. It is not possible to look at anything he designed without being almost crushed by the brilliantly organized, massive forms of building or object and by the crowded animation of the detail, whether it be the austere bulk of Castell Coch, so violently contrasting with the richness of the amazing rooms within, the symbol-encrusted interior of St Mary's, Studley Royal, a piece of church plate, gilded, bejewelled, inscribed and given a totally unexpected shape, or one of the architect's extraordinary beds, adorned with crystal balls, paintings, mirrors, illuminated vellum and fragments of textiles. And if the work itself is riveting, it is of exceptional interest in its context. For Burges presents a peculiarly sympathetic case of an artist stubbornly managing to exist and to realize himself in unpromising conditions.

In an expanding, industrialized society architect and craftsman had become irrevocably divorced. Standards of execution were falling as quantity was preferred to quality; the accent was on economics, and the speculative builder had come into his own. When Burges, who was first articled to Edward Blore, became Matthew Digby Wyatt's assistant in 1849 at the age of twenty-two, it had not yet become necessary for a man of genius to pass an examination before he could design a building; but the conflict between the profession and the art of architecture was already implicit in the social emphasis placed on the architect's professional standing, in the replacement of the 'patron' by the 'client', and in the transformation of the architect into a business man (a president of the Royal Society of British Architects defined him as 'a man of affairs') working in a large office, surrounded by draughtsmen frantically keeping up with a time-table. The architect was further faced with the antitheseis of architecture as an art and as a structural science. The Institute of Civil Engineers had come into being as early as 1818 and had received its Royal Charter in 1828. Although at first there was no conscious rivalry between architect and engineer the economic advantage of factory-made buildings ensured the eventual triumph of the engineer in the architectural field and relegated the architect in his true rôle of artist to a minor position. The situation was prefigured in the partnership of Brunel and M. D. Wyatt in the building of Paddington Station. Brunel saw himself as the principal partner, who was 'to build a station after my own fancy', while Wyatt was fitted for nothing more than the 'detail of ornamentation for which I have neither the time nor knowledge'.

Burges, as Wyatt's assistant, and as the son of an extremely successful engineer, was fully aware of the predicament. His own work proves that he commanded the basic constructional principles with more virtuosity than most engineers, but he only once made use of the engineer's materials – in the Speech Room he designed for Harrow School, where the pillars supporting the wooden roof are of cast iron. But these are no more related to the engineer's prefabrications than are the cast iron palms in the kitchen of the Royal Pavilion at Brighton. Burges's prolific articles in *The Gentleman's Magazine, The Building News* and *The Builder*, and the lectures he delivered at the Royal Institute of British Architects in 1864 on *Art Applied to Industry*, stress the importance of traditional materials. In the lectures Burges also advocates the close collaboration of the artist with the commercial firms carrying out his designs, to counteract the tendency for personal statements of striking quality to be vulgarized in the mass-produced pastiches of manufacturers. Burges always supervised the execution of every detail of his own decorative schemes.

He was not only alive to the practical difficulties confronting an architect: his career shows that he also realized the confusion of thought which equated Christianity and Gothic and, in an age dominated by the pursuit of wealth, proclaimed the identity of beauty and a rigidly doctrinaire religion, which was itself being ceaselessly undermined by the discoveries of science. Burges chose to remain aloof from the moral aspect of the Revival, and while he was closely connected with the Ecclesiological Society for reasons of convenience, he never pretended to subscribe to its eager dogmatism. His preference for Gothic had nothing to do with its supposed 'sacramentality'. 'There are some people', he wrote, 'who consider Medieval art as eminently ecclesiastical, and therefore something profoundly serious and to be approached with caution, forgetting that mankind has always been very much the same in every age, and that our ancestors joked and laughed just as much as we do.' Burges's medievalism was inspired by visual passion, an instinctive aversion to the classical mode, and unusual knowledge irradiated by the imagination of a genius.

Though he avoided the pitfall, which was the undoing of many of his contemporaries, of attempting to serve two gods, Burges could not change the attitudes and aims of his age, nor escape the undercurrent of anxiety induced by the ugliness and menacing potentialities of the industrial landscape. Like his friends Rossetti, Godwin and Burne-Jones he reacted against the philistine blizzard by creating a dream world, though of a very different character from the enfeebled, etherealized Pre-Raphaelite dream.

With his thoroughly practical appreciation of the chances of realizing his dream, Burges resolved, after a very short stay with Matthew Digby Wyatt, and after extended travels in France, Germany, Belgium and Italy had confirmed his preference for foreign Gothic of the thirteenth century, to work independently. Fortunately, with a comfortable income from his father, he could afford to dispense with a large practice. He must have known that it would not be easy to find patrons who would finance his elaborate, gigantic ideas, and this may have been the reason why he sought to make a name for himself by entering competitions. In 1855 he and Henry Clutton, a fellow pupil of Edward Blore, submitted a design for the Lille Cathedral competition and won it. But their plans were unfairly rejected in favour of a project by three Frenchmen. Burges suffered another rebuff in the following year when his design won the competition for the Crimea Memorial Church on the Bosphorus, for the committee refused to pay the cost of the stone vaulting, which was essential to the architect's conception. Later, in 1867, Burges's wonderfully romantic, scenic entry for the Law Courts competition was turned down as 'eccentric and wild' though 'his architecture exceeded in merit that of any other competitor'. Burges's resilient spirits were equal to the disappointment, and he gave no sign of resentment other than to remark about the winner's, Street's, style of drawing: 'What a pity that he cannot build his cross-hatching.' His own conceit, stormily lit in the drawing, with a tremendous tower in its north-west corner frowning upon the Strand, and a central castle with a vaulted hall, is more like an apocryphal vision of the power of law than a viable scheme, for Burges omitted essential requirements from his plan, and indeed it is marked, as the criticism of the design suggests, by a significant disregard for the limits of rationality. This was of the very nature of the architect's dream.

Meanwhile he had sent in designs for the Cork Cathedral competition of 1863. He won it, and this time work went ahead without impediment: the building was completed by 1876. The grandiose scheme could never have been carried out for the available sum of £15,000, but the Cork authorities, fired by Burges's enthusiasm and seduced by his charm, raised more money. St Finbar's embodies the salient characteristics of Burges's remarkable art: superb mastery of weight and volume is combined with a burden of ornamental fretwork which, minutely charged with symbolic and narrative meaning, is pursued with tireless energy and invention, but never (and this is singular in a period in which the greatest triumphs in every sphere were so often flawed by the sacrifice of the whole to proliferating detail) at the expense of form. Flaunting finials and crockets on every ridge, crowned by three massive spired towers, embellished with arcading, reliefs and statues set in dazzling fields of blue and gold mosaic or sheltered by vaulted canopies topped by little fortresses, the Cathedral glows with a vitality never found in the cold, unengaging compositions of such of Burges's doctrinaire and liturgically-minded contemporaries as Street and Butterfield. But looking at it through the sober urned gateway, relic of the century Burges referred to as the 'Dark Ages', there is a disquieting hint of the monstrous in that gigantic bulk bursting out of its very confined site, and more than a suggestion of the grotesque in the outrageous size of the carved symbols of the Evangelists round the great rose window.

There is the same conjunction of nobly conceived forms and aggressive proportions in the east wall of Waltham Abbey, which Burges restored from 1860 onwards. A band of reliefs, carved, like the sculpture at Cork, by the gifted Thomas Nicholls, and profusely gilded, serves not only as a reredos, but as the base of a composition of triple lancets and a wheel window of such weight, vehemence and grossness, even, that the grand Norman interior into which it is thrust can hardly contain it.

Burges's emphasis on exaggerated size intensifies the dream character of his architecture and underlines its affinities, despite the author's scholarship, with the Picturesque building of an earlier generation, one of the attributes of which was the cult of the colossal, declared by Burke to be an indispensable quality of the sublime. With Burges it is a way of keeping the contemporary world at a distance and of turning a vision into solid, material fact.

After the superabundant detail of the exterior of St Finbar's, the comparatively plain surfaces of the mighty interior come as a surprise. As Burges developed he reversed the contrast, concealing behind sparsely decorated, formally organized blocks of masonry some of the most exotic, luxuriant rooms ever devised. The outside of St Mary's, Studley Royal, built for Lord Ripon, is enlivened by pinnacles and an arrestingly original east window where statues merge with the vigorous tracery. But the relative restraint of the other elevations gives additional force to the astounding interior, where glittering, jewel-like ornament overspreads every surface, and the startling introduction of a coved, arcaded ceiling and a saucer dome distinguish the chancel.

Despite the attraction of the colour and costly substance of 'orphreyed baudekins, and pix and pax and chrismatory . . . and thurible and cross', the romance of religion was not for Burges. The habitat, the refuge he sought to create, was to take shape in the domestic field. It was here that the drama of his explosive conceits and contrasts reached its climax. Two of the houses for which he found congenial patrons, Knightshayes in Devon and Gayhurst in Buckinghamshire, give only a partial glimpse of the intended effect. Scarcely a trace remains of the great bedizened rooms once hidden behind the grotesquely inflated, dauntingly severe version of the traditional hall-house which is Knightshayes. And at Gayhurst, where Burges added a service wing to an Elizabethan house for Lord Carrington, the exciting group of preposterous, exhilaratingly unfunctional, magnificently massed, circular, rectangular and polygonal forms can no longer be seen in proximity to more than a few relics of the architect's dynamic transformations of Lord Carrington's interiors.

Burges's vision was, however, completely and gloriously made reality in the Welsh castles he rehabilitated and redesigned for the Marquess of Bute. Though twenty years divided the two men, and though one was austere, reserved and devout while the other was jovial, quick-witted and loquacious, patron and architect were united in their antiquarian delight in the Middle Ages and their rejection of Victorian materialism. Both had reacted against their fathers: one, as I have mentioned, an engineer, the other, though of aristocratic descent, an industrialist who had employed Burges senior to construct the East Bute Dock which turned the small port of Cardiff into a vast commercial city. The young Lord Bute, who was the inspiration for Disraeli's *Lothair*, and was generally attired in the habit of a monk, was a millionaire, and spared no expense to realize the medieval escape dream Burges devised for them both. Cardiff Castle and Castell Coch stand out among all the Victorian fancy-dress country houses in having been conceived from the first as places of dream. These castles were not seriously intended as houses to live in: they were of the same wholly irrational order as the fairy palaces built under Wagner's influence by Ludwig II in the Bavarian mountains. Many Victorian buildings translate reality into fantasy – a railway station and a museum become cathedrals, and a dairy the chapter house of a 'monastic farm'. But Lord Bute's castles are fantasies made fact, vivid with a realism which is something like hallucination.

Both buildings stand on the sites of earlier fortresses. The remains of Cardiff Castle consisted of a huge shell keep, along one side of which was a range of medieval lodgings to which Capability Brown had given a few Gothic flourishes. It was this range that Burges transfigured by his unique, fiercely concentrated interpretation of the medieval theme. Much of the character of the spurned design for the Law Courts has materialized in the powerful, irregular silhouette of this turretted ca tle, with its upstarting verticals all dominated by the great top-heavy clock tower. Yet the general robust impression is not so much romantic as abstract, despite the huge, ridiculous sculptured animals peering over the curtain wall. These monumental expressions of irrepressible vitality and a high-mettled scorn of 'taste' recall Dickens's similar liberating lapses into vulgarity, just as the fantasy and strangeness flowering from Burges's stupendous architecture in the form of teeming, often whimsical detail have their parallels in the novelist's predilection for minutely experienced, crowded scenes restlessly sprouting into outcrops of ever more detail.

No such outbreak of boisterous spirits disturbs the bold exterior geometry and fine simplicity of Castell Coch on its eminence above the River Taffy. The stout, cylindrical towers are adorned only by their roof-cones, which, conspicuously foreign, stamp this overpoweringly solid and plausible evocation of an impregnable stronghold with a calculated air of make-believe.

At both Cardiff and Castell Coch the outward aspect of the building gives no inkling of the incredible, secret riches within. The hugeness and the sense of multitudinousness are shattering. Amid all the bulging, flowing, burgeoning ornament, gorgeous colour, bizarre shapes and proportions, it is perhaps the fantastic fireplaces, one taking the form of a castle with figures waving and blowing trumpets from the battlements, and the unforgettable, grossly corrugated ceilings, carved with deep coffers, domes, star-shaped designs and curiously swollen, banded mouldings like horizontal columns, that first attract attention. Then, as the spectator begins to assimilate the overspilling detail, he is spellbound not only by the almost maniacal thoroughness and zest of the execution but by its character. The author of this riot of chimerical figures with streaming hair, of dragons, reptilian creatures and mocking fiends, of birds, monkeys and rodents and exquisite plant forms, is, like Shakespeare, a master of the double plot, specializing in contrast: beauty and the beast. And the demonic vigour is offset by comic verve.

The culmination of it all is the Summer Smoking Room at the top of the Clock Tower. On entering this gold and dusky red apartment the visitor is instantly struck by its violently un-classical proportions. The walls and squat columns supporting a steep cove and a balcony of gilded ironwork with a dome above it are scarcely a quarter of the height of the lofty chamber. All the ornament illustrates a single theme, that of the firmament and the earth below it. A vast chandelier crowned by a gleaming Apollo-like figure takes the form of sunrays whose light is refracted and magnified in the mirror lining the dome over-head. Immediately underneath the chandelier shines a bronze model of the world encircled by enamelled tiles depicting the spheres. Compelling figures set between the shafts of the gar-gantuan angle columns and the exaggerated coils of the capitals symbolize the winds coming from the four corners of the earth and are carved with such force that they seem to be hurling themselves from the pillars. Upon the hooded chimneypiece sits Cupid with parrots (Burges's favourite bird) on his wrists, while the frieze below him shows summer lovers and the state of matrimony represented by two dogs pulling in opposite directions and a dog barking at a cat in a tree. The capitals of the pillars are painted with portraits of the great astronomers.

It is typical of this dream room that it should command a giddily aerial prospect of Cardiff and the docks, the Bristol Channel and the Welsh mountains. The distant view and dizzy exaltation accentuate the remoteness of the strange apartment. The top room at Castell Coch, looking down into a misty land-scape of valley, hill and sea, is yet further removed from everyday reality. The very shape of the room, circular and roofed by a great curved dome, encloses and insulates.

It is Lady Bute's bedchamber, though no one ever slept in it; and in Burges's vision, concentrating on dream and night, it assumes greater importance than any other apartment in the castle. Subdued light falls on colours of dull gold, clear red and willow green and on enchanting naturalistic foliage coiling about the dome and peopled by birds and monkeys. A gentle, tender background, the more to enhance the oddity and flamboyance of the great bed with its glitter of glass balls and the fantasy dressing table and washstand disguised as castles.

The decoration of this marvellously atmospheric room was completed only after Burges's premature death in April 1881. He did not live to enjoy the Tower House refuge and shrine he had built for himself. Like Castell Coch it secretes precious rooms, studded, bejewelled and encrusted with story-telling devices behind a severe assembly of cylinder and rectangle; and like Castell Coch it reaches a pitch of exultance in its fabulous bed-chambers and legendary beds. The figure of Fame is the tutelary deity of Burges's house. Holding a sceptre and a crystal ball, bronze, with face and hands of ivory and with sapphires for eyes, she stands on one of the richest chimneypieces, a fitting symbol of the fulfilment of her creator's aspirations. It is Burges's special achievement to have given form to his burningly idiosyncratic imaginings without any sacrifice of artistic scruple, and never to have been deflected by false morality and false sentiment. His art was by force of circumstance one man deep. Even though he created a new and brilliantly stimulating architecture in the traditional language of Gothic, he could have no followers. Nothing could come of an escape from the present into an ideal of make-believe: a new science of building morphology was at hand to accord with the accelerating materialism of the mass culture Burges abhorred.

The Fantasy World of Sidney Sime

BY JOHN LEWIS

WITH PHOTOGRAPHS BY JOHN WEBB

'WE HAVE LOST, in a time of losses, when loss is nothing out of the ordinary, a genius whose stupendous imagination has passed across our time little more noticed by most people than the shadow of a bird. . . . There was in his pictures a sombre grandeur showing all the majesty of night, or the mystery of dark forests, or the hair-raising spells which won your credulity.' This was Lord Dunsany's tribute to Sidney Herbert Sime which appeared in *The Fortnightly Review*. Sime had died on May 22, 1941. His death passed almost unnoticed. Dunsany of course remembered him, for Sime had illustrated a number of Dunsany's books, and Dunsany in his turn had written at least one book, or the major part of one book, around Sime's drawings. But for the last quarter of a century of his life Sime had virtually disappeared from public view.

Yet at the turn of the century S. H. Sime was one of the most famous of living black-and-white artists. It was the age of the magazine: *Punch, Pick-me-up, The Idler, The Butterfly, The Illustrated London News, The Sketch, The Strand, The Pall Mall Magazine* and so on. Sime's work appeared in all of these. He first made his name as a theatrical cartoonist, but his fame was to rest on his drawings of 'the shades'. These were pictures of murky forests, sulphurous caves and other benighted regions. In all these doom-laden drawings there was some slight jolting piece of reality, such as a very mundane common-or-garden stove pipe appearing out of some horrific demon's lair. He drew so vividly that if he was drawing a charwoman scrubbing some gargantuan steps, which turned out to be made of soap, he made one believe in the fantasy because of the reality of the little woman.

Sidney Sime was born in Manchester in 1867. His family was very poor, and at an early age, with practically no schooling, he was sent to work in the coal mines. He worked for five years below ground and formed such a close relationship with the pit pony which pulled his 'scoop' that when he left the mine the pony refused to work for anyone else. The boy Sime used to scratch drawings of demons on the coalface, which the manager of the pit would show to his friends with some pride.

After his spell below ground Sidney Sime worked for a draper, a baker and a shoemaker before becoming apprenticed to a signwriter. Before he was out of his teens he found time to attend classes at the Liverpool School of Art. In 1888 he won the prize for life drawing, a copy of Tennyson's *Poems*, and soon afterwards he won one of the South Kensington medals for drawing – 'an award that was always considered a hall-mark of the duffer', he later remarked. He then began a career as a free-lance illustrator working for the halfpenny comic papers. By 1892 Sime's drawings had appeared in several London magazines including a full page in *The Illustrated London News*. With this success he set out for London in the following year. He was a fluent draughtsman and had little difficulty in placing his drawings in magazines as different as *The Boy's Own Paper* and *The Illustrated Sporting and Dramatic News*.

Sime's first real break-through came in 1895. L. Raven Hill, the editor of *Pick-me-up*, who was himself a superb draughtsman, recognized the Manchester boy's talent and offered him regular work. *Pick-me-up* (in spite of its name) was a first-class paper and a worthy rival to *Punch*. In 1896 Raven Hill asked Sime if he would illustrate the amusing theatre criticisms of Arnold Golsworthy.

Sime's theatrical caricatures are worthy of a study on their own. It has been said that he was not particularly interested in this work. Be that as it may, he took it seriously enough. He often visited a play three or four times to assimilate the characters of those he was drawing. He found the conditions of having to draw in the darkness of the auditorium and the inquisitive interest of people sitting on either side of him somewhat tiresome. The drawings he made then were little more than *aides mémoires*. As well as being a fine draughtsman, Sime was gifted

A caricature of Marie Lloyd by Sidney Sime

with a marvellous visual memory and when illustrating never
worked from models. This is probably true of most good illustrators. William Heath Robinson, an avowed admirer of Sime,
stated that he also never used models for his drawings.

Sime's theatrical drawings have much more to them than the
usual caricatures of stage personalities. They set the scene and,

particularly with the music hall drawings, show something of the vulnerability of those figures isolated under spotlights and fighting to win over what may well have been a hostile, half-empty house.

In 1898 Sidney Sime married Mary Susan Pickett, an attractive Edinburgh girl who was an accomplished miniature painter. To the end of his life she remained his most loyal admirer. In the same year as he was married an uncle died, leaving Sidney Sime a small fortune and a large well-furnished house at Aberfoyle in Perthshire. Sime was at that time earning about £1,000 a year, so he now found himself very comfortably off. On the strength of his new-found wealth he bought a little magazine called *The Idler*, for which he had been doing some drawings. He installed a journalist called Arthur Lawrence as editor. Lawrence in fact had interviewed Sime for *The Idler* in the previous January.

For the next few years Sime spent six months of each year in Scotland, living in the house at Aberfoyle and painting the highland scenery. These paintings and pastel drawings are both personal and decorative, though at that time they did nothing to further his reputation. His drawings of Heaven and Hell that were appearing in the magazines took care of that.

Sime's excursion into magazine publishing was rather costly. *The Idler*, when he bought it, was in fact in a sinking condition with a load of debts that had been skilfully concealed from him. In 1901 Sime cut his losses and sold the goodwill of the magazine for £5. It would seem that though he must have lost much of his capital in the venture he was still earning a good income from his illustration work.

In 1905 the American newspaper tycoon, William Randolph Hearst, invited Sime to the United States. Sime worked there for six months. His drawings were so successful that Hearst offered him a retainer of £800 a year if he would remain. In spite of this tempting offer, Sime felt his success in London was assured. Also he missed his friends at the Yorick Club and the Langham Sketch Club.

So Sime returned to England, and as the house in Perthshire, empty for half the year, was something of a liability, he sold it, and after some searching found and bought a pretty, rambling old cottage in the village of Worplesdon near Guildford in Surrey. It had a stable which he converted into a studio.

So Sime's work was almost entirely for magazines. His only book illustrations were for a series of books by Lord Dunsany. The first of these was *The Gods of Pegana*, which Elkin Matthews published in 1905. For this book Sime made eight drawings. He was immediately in sympathy with Lord Dunsany's ideas. The two men, from such diffcrent backgrounds, found they had much in common. Dunsany said 'Sime's was a great brain. Few illustrators have had his extensive mental range and his stupendous imagination.'

Everyone who met Sime and who recorded impressions of him remarked on the power of his mind. Holbrook Jackson, writing about Sime in his book *The Eighteen-Nineties* in 1913, said: 'Few artists of the time had his versatility, and still fewer his mental range.' In 1922 Haldane McFall wrote, somewhat ecstatically, in *The Illustrated London News*: 'There is not one brain of all those that sleep that could compare with the brain of this man; not one poet of them all gifted with such poetic lyricism as that of Sidney Sime.'

As for his appearance, Frank Harris describes Sime as: 'a strongly built man of about five foot seven or five foot eight, with a cliff-like overhanging tyrannous forehead; his grey eyes are superlative, greyish blue looking out under heavy brows, eyes with a pathetic patience in them as of one who has lived with sorrow.' James Thorpe, the *Punch* artist and art historian, in an unpublished manuscript about Sime, wrote in 1948: 'My earliest memory of Sime, forty years ago at the Langham Sketch Club conversazione, is of a slim figure, slightly above average height with a rather large head crowned with a thick mop of black hair . . . his expression was sardonic with a smile always playing round his mouth. He had a thin black beard which grew in two points. Someone has said that he only wanted two short horns to resemble those little figures of devils which he drew so often.' On Max Beerbohm saying to him: 'It must be wonderful, Sime, to look like nothing else on earth', Sime went straight home and shaved off his beard. As he grew older, he grew plumper in the face, less sardonic in expression.

That Sime was a man of parts there can be no question. With virtually no formal education, he was very well read, and late in life taught himself both Latin and Greek. Meredith was his favourite novelist and he made an exhaustive study of Blake's works. He was a brilliant conversationalist and could hold his own with anyone. In 1919 he was staying with the Dunsanys in Ireland. Beatrice Dunsany, in a letter to a friend, wrote: 'Mr Sime stayed here for a week . . . he is *very* nice, most interesting . . . his conversation that of a scholar and a philosopher, his interest and knowledge vast and varied.' H. G. Wells was also staying at Dunsany Castle. Lady Dunsany remarked 'When Sime and Wells really got going, it was a joy to listen.'

So much for the man and what his contemporaries thought of him. Of his work, the drawings of Heaven and Hell and the intermediate regions of after life may owe some of their origins to the time he was working in a coal mine. As a young artist he was influenced by Beardsley and by Hokusai and Hiroshige. (He had a large collection of Japanese prints.) There is another quite different element in his work and that is Symbolism. The key to this observation lies in an article on Odilon Redon by P. G. Konody in *The Idler* of April 1900. Drawings by Sime appeared in the same issue. Konody wrote: 'Odilon Redon is the illustrator *par excellence* of decadent poetry and literature . . . the gruesome monsters by which his world is peopled, the grinning skulls and fiendish countenances, which seem to peer through the impenetrable darkness . . .' He might have been writing about Sime with these last words. The essence of Symbolism was to suggest reality, not to depict it literally. Sime once said: 'Art does not lie in performance; it is a mental condition.' Sime used dreams for inspiration and created visionary images in terms of black and white as did Odilon Redon; but, unlike the French Symbolist, to relieve the sombre scenes there were frequent flashes of humour.

For the first thirty years of his career, apart from his Scottish landscape paintings, Sime worked like Redon in monochrome, in charcoal, lamp black and Indian ink. Again, like Redon, as he grew older he began to paint fantastic landscapes in encrusted and irridescent colours that remind one of the paintings of Gustave Moreau.

Sime continued to illustrate Lord Dunsany's books, ten of them in all. In *The Sword of Welleran* Lord Dunsany introduced a Sime drawing of three sinister figures approaching a gibbet, from which hangs the putrefying corpse of a highwayman, with these words: 'Their names were Joe and Will and the Gipsy Puglioni . . . sin had caressed their faces . . . their food was robbery and their pastime murder.' This drawing had actually appeared in *The Idler*, eight or nine years earlier under the title of 'The Hand of Glory' as an illustration to *The Ingoldsby Legends*. It would seem that Dunsany wrote his story round the drawing. He certainly used this method for ten of the stories in *The Book of Wonder* (1912). Author and artist were in perfect harmony. They were virtually interchangeable.

In 1914 Sime was forty-seven. Even so, he joined up and served with the Army Service Corps on the east coast. He was invalided out of the Army with a duodenal ulcer on Armistice Day in 1918. He returned to Worplesdon hoping to pick up his career where he had left off. He found his old connections in publishing had disappeared and new artists had arrived. At intervals his drawings appeared in *The Illustrated London News*, *The Tatler* or *The Sketch*. In 1920 he completed his last set of illustrations for Dunsany.

He gently and perhaps not too reluctantly retired into village life. He spent much time in his garden and even more in the local pub where he did a brilliant set of portrait drawings of the regular customers. And he painted coruscating fantasies in oil and scenes by moonlight and landscapes in a mosaic-like technique (these were in fact collages). Some of his paintings had curious crenellated skies. There were two successful exhibitions of Sime's work at the St George's Gallery in London in 1924 and 1927. He had his patrons, amongst whom were, apart from Lord Dunsany, Desmond Coke and Lord Howard de Walden, with whom he had worked on stage productions just before the First Great War.

Lord Dunsany last visited Sime in 1938, when he found him up to the neck in paper and drawings. It was clear that the Simes were hard up, though he was reasonably successful in backing horses! In 1940 Lord Dunsany wrote to Sir Kenneth Clark to see if it was possible to secure some kind of pension. He learned in reply that Sime was dying.

One of the fantasies in the Sime Gallery at Worplesdon

One of the fantastic paintings in the Sime Gallery at Worplesdon

The Hand of Glory,' an illustration to *The Ingoldsby Legends* in *The Idler*, later used to illustrate *The Sword of Welleran* by Lord Dunsany, with the title 'Tom o' the Roads'

'Rich man at the Gates of Heaven'

'Old Houses'

The Moonlighters

IN VIEW of the revival of interest in Victorian painting it is surprising that so little has been written about a once popular and distinctive school of minor nineteenth-century art, the 'moonlight painters', of whom the best-known were members of the Pether family. The father of the 'moonlighters' was Abraham Pether (1756–1812), a respected landscape painter now chiefly remembered as the painter of the moonlit church in the background of the *Temple of Flora* mezzotint of 'The Night-Blowing Cereus'. Abraham Pether was obviously influenced by the various moonlit landscapes painted by Joseph Wright of Derby, and he began to paint conventional eighteenth-century landscapes, employing moonlight effects (one of which is reproduced on page 220). Abraham's son Sebastian (1790–1844) is often described as copying his father's work, but in fact he was a more individual artist, who perfectly expressed the interest taken by the Romantic Movement in imaginery 'gothick' scenes – ruined abbeys and castles, waterfalls, and winding rivers.

A typically 'gothick' landscape by Sebastian Pether, signed with his initials and dated 1820. It measures 17½ × 16 inches, and has the characteristic green tinge on a sombre grey-brown background which marks Sebastian Pether's work. Opposite is a smaller, unsigned painting by Sebastian Pether (Collection of Mr and Mrs John Hadfield).

Nowadays the best-known member of the Pether family is Henry, who is variously described in works of reference as Sebastian's brother and his son. Certainly he was younger than Sebastian, since he exhibited at the Royal Academy between 1828 and 1862. The paintings definitely attributable to him, and signed by his full name in bold and angular, often backward-slanting script, are almost always identifiable scenes, realistically portrayed. Many of them show scenes on the Thames; others show scenes in Scotland, Venice or Paris. Always there is a moon, and water. They are painted rather thinly on the canvas, very smoothly, and in warm, brown tones, as distinct from the more metallic, green tones of Sebastian's paintings.

Apart from the paintings signed by Sebastian or Henry there are many 'moonlights', such as that illustrated above, bearing no signature. They are smoothly painted, brown in tone, usually on canvases measuring 24 × 29 inches. There is nearly always a ruined castle or abbey on the left, with a fairly large figure in a boat or on a bank in the foreground. Were they early work by Henry Pether, before he established his own style and reputation?

Two paintings signed by Henry Pether: above, Battersea Bridge, with Chelsea old church (Oscar and Peter Johnson), and below, Marlow on Thames (Richard Green)

H ERE ARE examples of moonlight paintings by the three
Pethers. Above is a conventional landscape, in eighteenth-
century style, by Abraham Pether, signed with his mono-
gram, measuring 14×18 inches. At the top of the page opposite is
an unsigned painting, measuring 19×24 inches, which is characteristic of the unsigned paintings now attributed to Henry Pether
(Collection of George Rainbird). It is smoothly painted; there is
a figure in the foreground; there is a boat in the middle distance.
Below, on the opposite page, is a typically Romantic 'moonlight',
signed with his initials by Sebastian Pether and dated 1822 (Collection of John Hadfield). The painting is rougher, with a
characteristic green tinge. The size is one frequently used by
Sebastian Pether (14×18 inches), and the elements of composition
are essentially gothick, with a light shining from a window in
the farm on the left, a series of waterfalls, and two small symbolic figures under the archway in the castle on the right.

The Ring of Glass

BY ALLAN STACEY

PHOTOGRAPHS BY JOHN W. R. BARROW

GLASS BELLS were made from about 1755 until the late nineteenth century and originally were the result of glass blowers using up oddments of glass left over at the end of the day and sold for pocket money. The shape of the bell can be likened to an upturned drinking glass, without a foot. I imagine that apprentices, before making them, would have practised their craft by blowing larger pieces, accustoming themselves to using their tools and working with molten glass. When turned upside down, these became handsome bells and an ideal shape for showing colour. The bells were made with an opening at the top forming a collar into which fitted the stump of the handle, secured with plaster. A looped piece of wire was inserted serving as a hook from which to hang a clapper.

There was a lull in output around the period of the Excise Act of 1777; then a renewal of interest caused some of the best examples to be produced from Bristol and Nailsea until 1783–4 when the use of plain glass for table ware took priority. The demand for coloured glass revived in the 1820s and there was an increasing output of glass bells from then onwards, London, Aberdeen, Stourbridge and other glass factors also producing them. After 1851, production reflected a more demanding market than could be satisfied by the personal fancy of individual glass blowers and caused a flow of plain bells to be produced.

Apart from sets, each bell handle is different. Some have an air twist or a cotton twist running from top to bottom. Another variation is a tear or bubble and some handles are hollow and decorated with festoons. The finial on the handle might have several rings of glass diminishing to a point, topped with an opaque bead, or be a twist of glass, like a flame.

Glass bells have increased in value and diminished in availability and the chance of finding an unusual specimen is a constant spur to the collector.

The left-hand bell is unusual in that the bell is of two colours, one half being blue and the other red, the twisted ribbons in the stem are red, white and blue. The small bell is cut, with an air twist in the handle. The large bell, 15″ tall, is festooned in white and has a hollow handle ornamented with clear glass curls indicating a Venetian influence. Period c.1780/1860

The large bell above on the left has pink, blue and white festoons which are repeated as ribbons in the handle. The rear centre bell above is orange and white and that in front of it is yellow and white. The bell on the right is spotted, red on white, sometimes called dalmatian. Period c.1755/1800.

On the top shelf in the colour plate opposite are two miniature bells and a spotted bell. On the shelf below, the centre bell is an eighteenth-century Bristol bell, and the penultimate one has a three-colour twist handle. The third shelf down shows four miniature bells, one cut, with an air twist handle; the last bell is dark purple. On the lower shelf the right-hand bell is amber and the one next to it has a blown handle decorated with *latticino*.

On the left above is an 'overlay' bell, red glass upon white, the finial is three hollow balls. The other two are white with a blue rim and an early Bristol blue with tears in the handle. The photograph shows a selection of clappers. Period c1755/85.

This is a set of three bells. Sets are most difficult to find, one or two having being broken at some time. These are cranberry coloured and are twisted, they have white rims and white handles, the finial ending in an opaque tear. Period c1830

THEN AND NOW

OTOGRAPHS CHOSEN BY MARY ANNE NORBURY

Above: Hyde Park, 1899 (*Saturday Book* Collection). Below: Hyde Park, 1974 (Topix)

Young Militant, 1920
(Ronald Grant
Collection)

Young Militant,
Ulster, 1972
(Press Association)

229

The Young Idea, 1880
(Ronald Grant Collection)

The Young Idea, 1965
(*Daily Mirror*)

230

Unchanging Eton: above, 1897 (*Saturday Book* Collection); below, 1974 (John Warwick)

Getting married, 1890 (Ronald Grant Collection)

Getting married, 1974 (Press Association)

Telephone Girls, 1896 and 1974
(Mander & Mitchenson Collection: Transworld)

The Strand,
London, 1895
(Radio Times
Hulton Library)
and 1974
(John Warwick)

236

Cycling, 1899
(Radio Times Hulton Library)

Cycling, 1974 (Keystone)

237

Above: Cricket in England, 1900 (Ronald Grant Collection)
Below: Cricket in Australia, 1974 (Patrick Eagar)

Above: Soccer crowd at Fulham, 1926 (Radio Times Hulton Library)
Below: Rugger crowd at Twickenham, 1974 (Syndication International)

Above: Riviera holiday at Cap d'Antibes, 1921 (Ronald Grant Collection)
Below: Riviera holiday on the Ile de Levant, 1973